Let's draw
DINOSAURS
pterodactyls and other prehistoric creatures

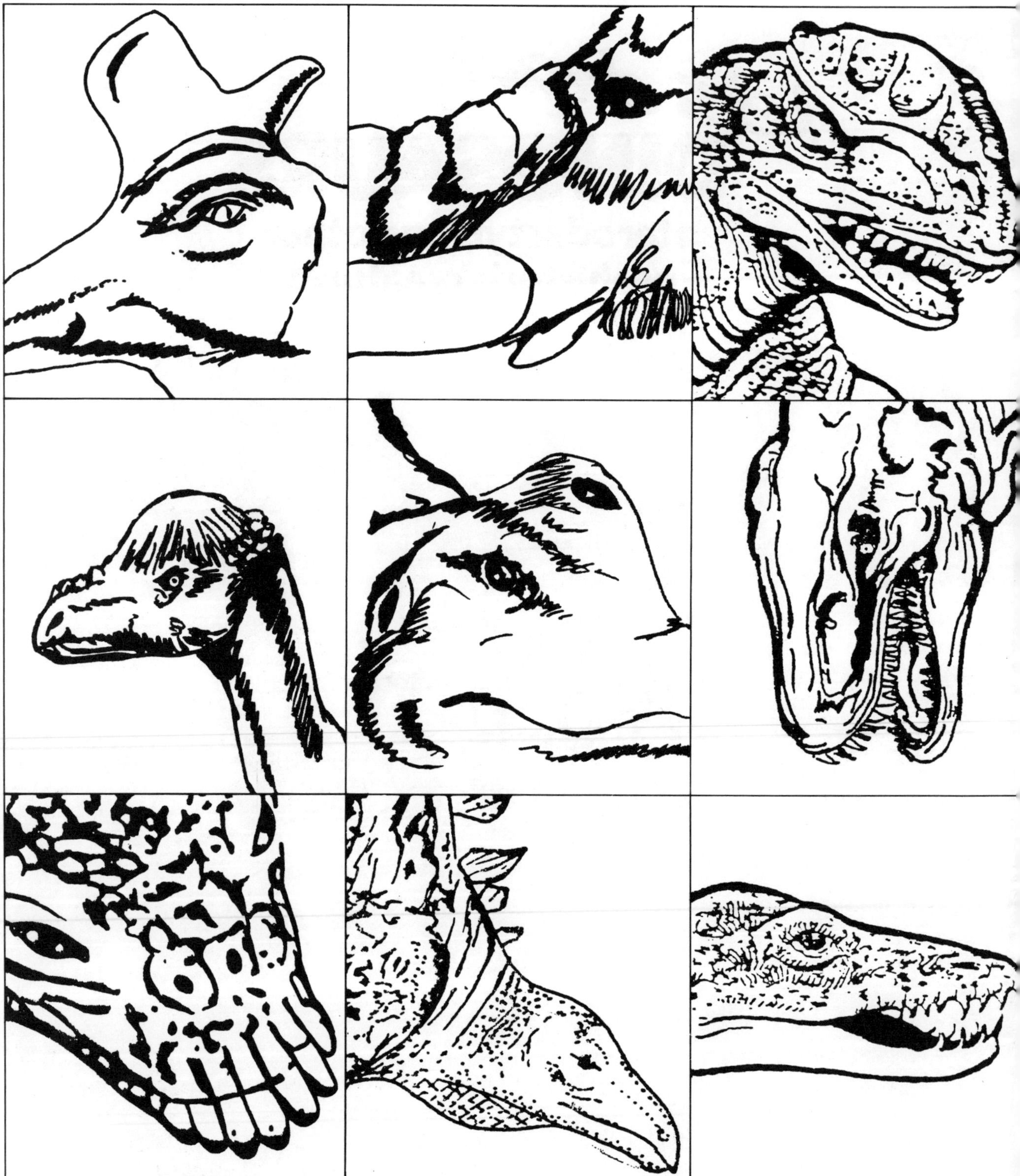

Here and at the back of the book are details from some of the drawings featured. Can you find the pages on which they appear?

Also in this series:

LET'S DRAW CARS
trucks and other vehicles

LET'S DRAW CATS
dogs and other animals

LET'S DRAW MONSTERS
ghosts, ghouls and demons

LET'S DRAW DINOSAURS, PTERODACTYLS AND OTHER PREHISTORIC CREATURES

Illustrations by
Darren Bennett, Michael Bentley, Ryozo Kohira, Kathleen McDougall, Philip Patenall, Bruce Robertson, Jane Robertson, Graham Rosewarne, Tim Scrivens, Dino Skeete

© Diagram Visual Information Ltd 1990

All rights reserved including the right of reproduction in whole or in part in any form

First published in Great Britain in 1990
by Simon & Schuster Young Books

Simon & Schuster Young Books
Simon & Schuster International Group
Wolsey House
Wolsey Road
Hemel Hempstead HP2 4SS

Typeset by Bournetype, Bournemouth, England
Printed and bound by Snoeck Ducaju & Sons, Ghent, Belgium

British Library Cataloguing in Publication data
Robertson, Bruce *1934–*
    Dinosaurs, pterodactyls and other prehistoric creatures.
    1. Drawings. Techniques
    I. Title II. Series
    741.2
    ISBN 0-7500-0226-3

Let's draw
DINOSAURS
pterodactyls and other prehistoric creatures

Bruce Robertson

Text by Sue Pinkus

SIMON & SCHUSTER

LONDON • SYDNEY • NEW YORK • TOKYO • SINGAPORE • TORONTO

About this book

Dinosaurs and other prehistoric creatures that lived millions of years ago are great fun to draw. It may look difficult, but this book will show you how easy it is to create fabulous pictures that really bring these extinct creatures to life again.

Pages 8–17

THE DINOSAUR STORY

First, in **Part 1**, discover where and when dinosaurs lived and what they looked like. They were not all the same, as you will see. (They are also called by names that are sometimes hard to say if you do not know them. So we have given you clues to help with this.)

Pages 18–45

GETTING READY TO DRAW

In **Part 2**, find out all you need to know about using pencils, chalks, felt-tips, ballpoint pens, brushes, paints, crayons and other tools like a real artist.

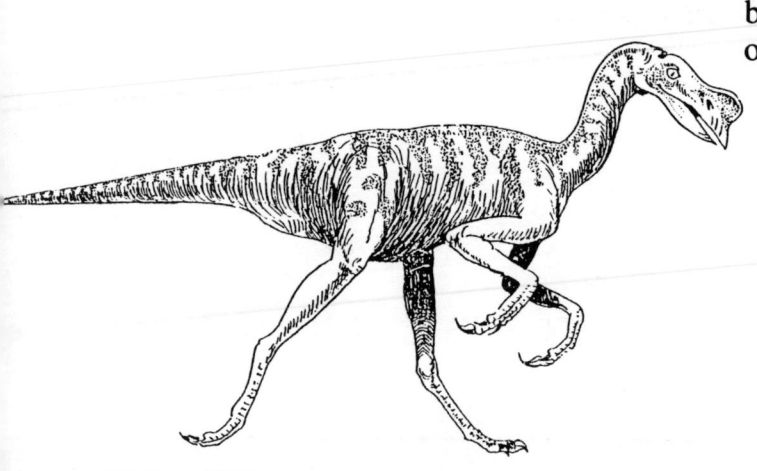

Enjoy making lots of wonderful dinosaur pictures! You'll find some great ideas for things to do with your drawings when you have finished them, too.

As you can see, this book has large page numbers. They are there to help you find your way easily to a drawing you might need to look at again while you are working.

Pages 46–63

DRAWING DINOSAURS IS EASY!

Part 3 tells you how to draw all sorts of dinosaurs in step-by-step stages. Start with just a few circles, ovals and lines, and you will soon have a picture of a **Diplodocus** (dip-low-doh-kus) like the one on page 75. It's as simple as that!

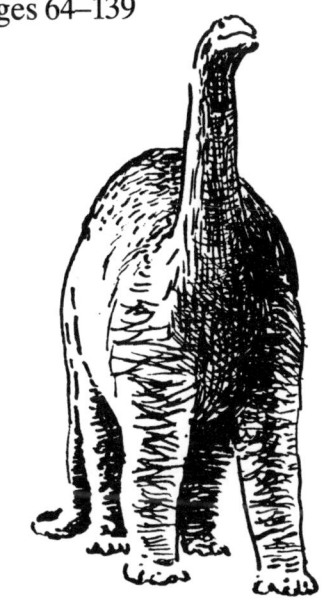

Pages 64–139

YOUR DINOSAUR GALLERY

In **Part 4**, there's a whole picture gallery of dinosaurs for you to look at and copy. And there are lots of expert hints and special tips, too.

©DIAGRAM

Part 1

This is a picture of a **Probactrosaurus** (proh-back-troh-saw-rus) from China. You can see its skeleton here, too. It usually walked on all-fours. But when it reared up on its hind legs, it was three times as tall as a full grown man.

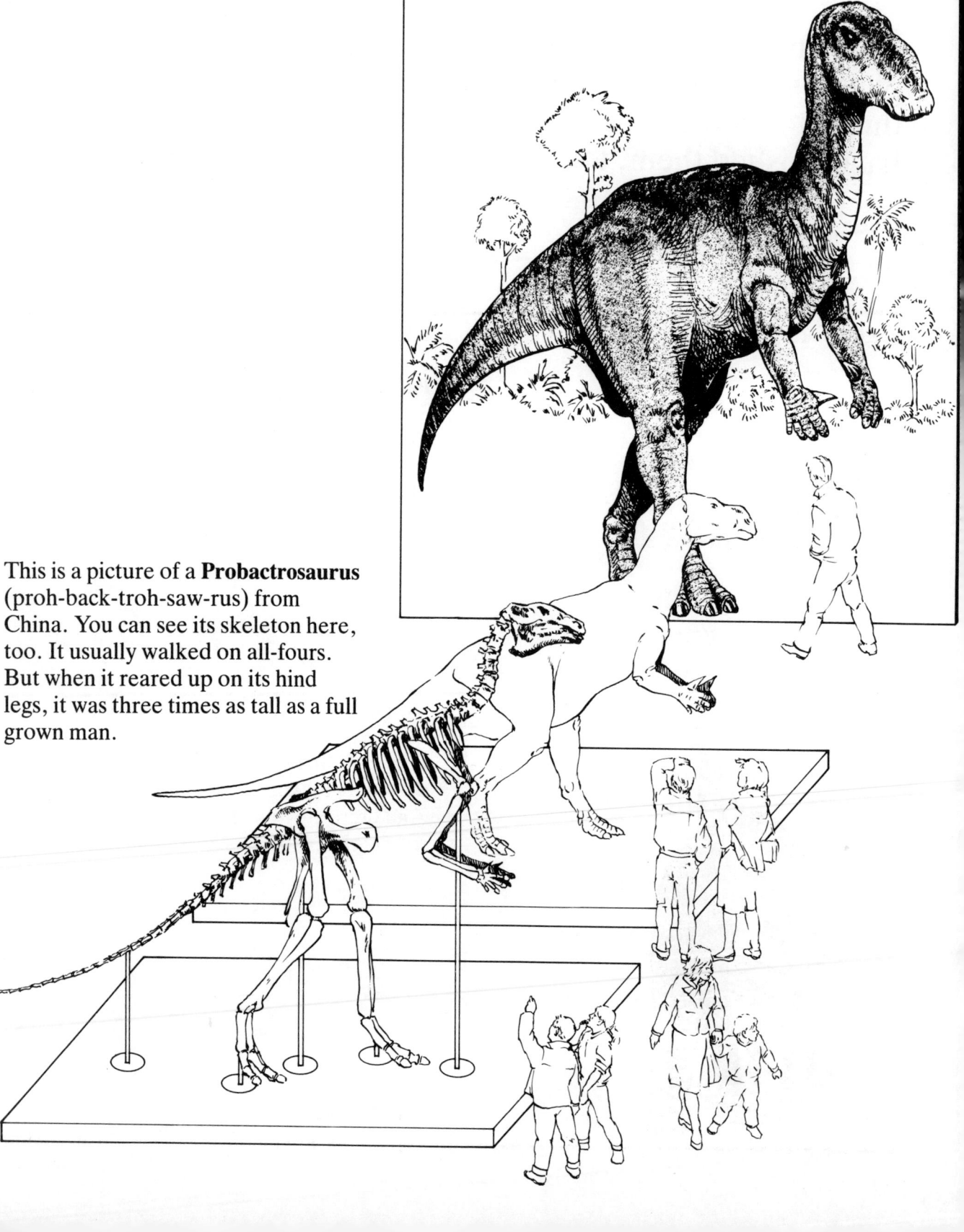

THE DINOSAUR STORY

Imagine the world millions of years ago. It was a strange, wild place. There were murky swamps, dense forests, grasslands and huge desert areas. Everywhere you could hear the terrifying sound of gigantic monsters – dinosaurs.

No one has ever seen a real dinosaur. They died out millions of years before the first human beings lived. But we know a lot about them from fossils that have been dug up. Bones, claws, teeth and even footprints have been found in places like Africa, Mongolia and the Midwest of America.

Scientists have also added pieces to the dinosaur bits they have found. In this way they have built life-size skeletons which you can see in many museums around the world or in photographs and drawings. Some of the most exciting models have also been made to move and growl.

This part of the book takes a look at when and where dinosaurs lived, what they ate and what they looked like.

Come dinosaur-hunting! Find out all about these amazing creatures on the pages that follow before you start drawing them.

©DIAGRAM

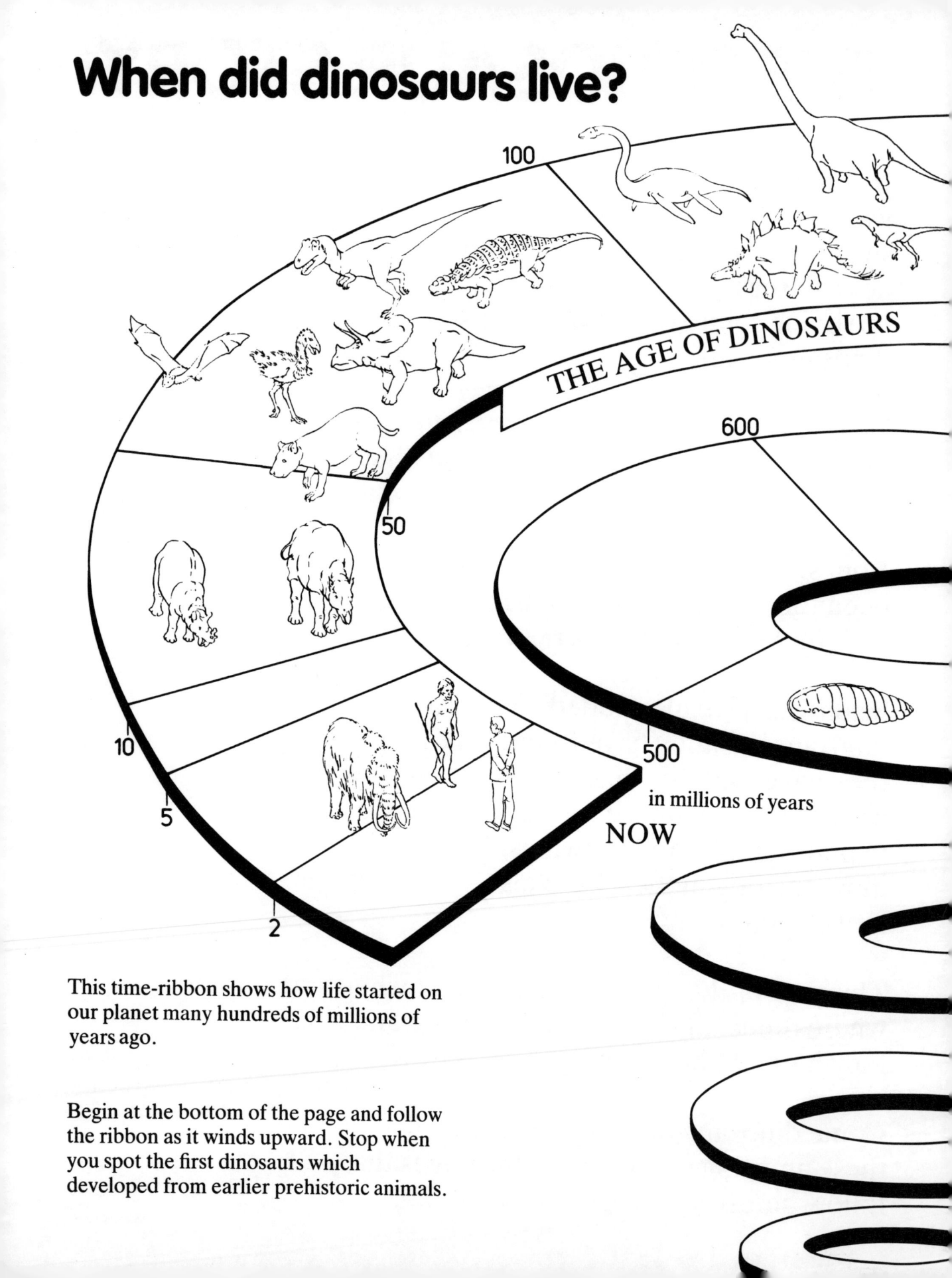

When did dinosaurs live?

THE AGE OF DINOSAURS

100
600
50
500
in millions of years
NOW
10
5
2

This time-ribbon shows how life started on our planet many hundreds of millions of years ago.

Begin at the bottom of the page and follow the ribbon as it winds upward. Stop when you spot the first dinosaurs which developed from earlier prehistoric animals.

11

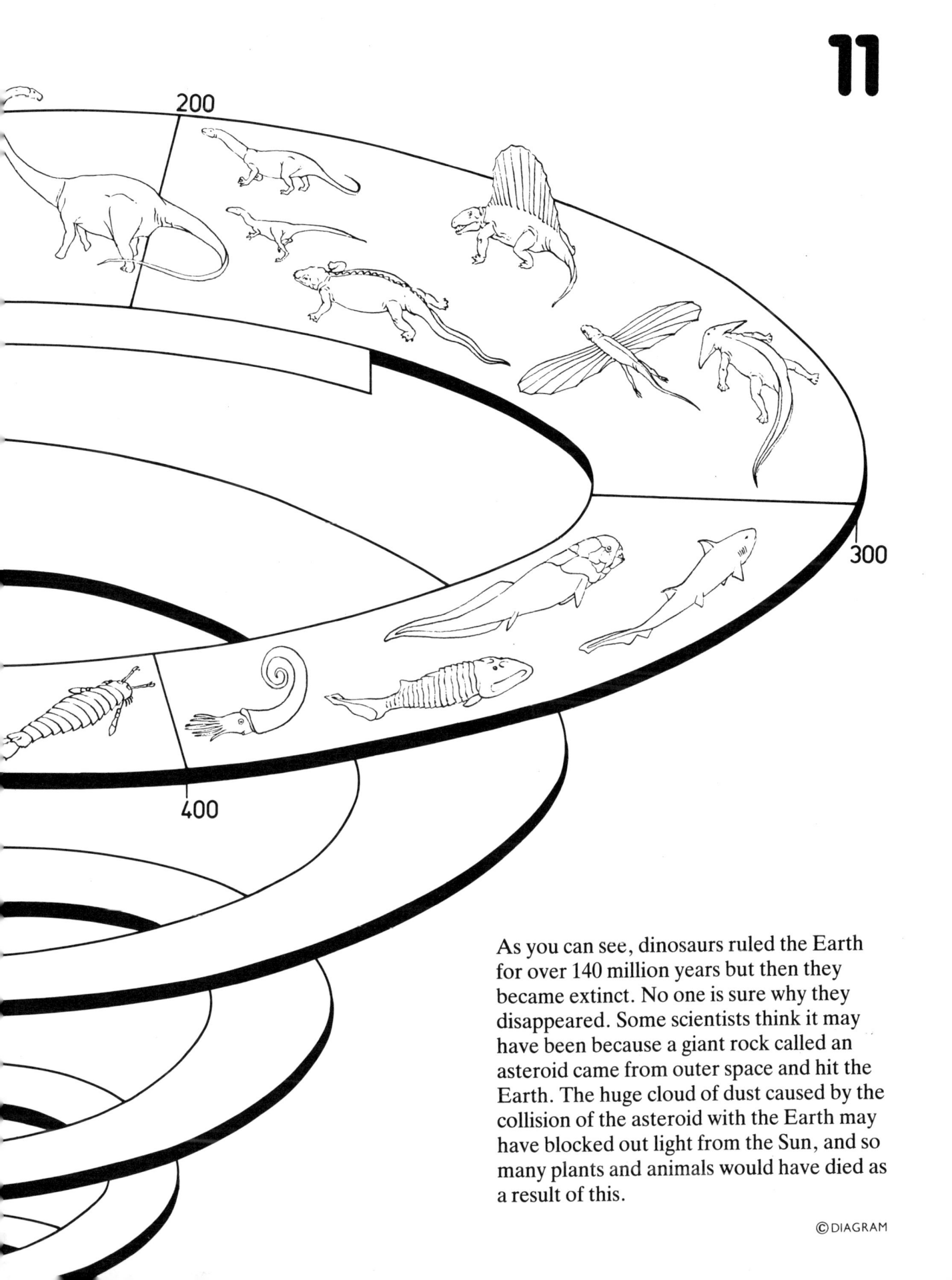

200

300

400

As you can see, dinosaurs ruled the Earth for over 140 million years but then they became extinct. No one is sure why they disappeared. Some scientists think it may have been because a giant rock called an asteroid came from outer space and hit the Earth. The huge cloud of dust caused by the collision of the asteroid with the Earth may have blocked out light from the Sun, and so many plants and animals would have died as a result of this.

©DIAGRAM

What were dinosaurs like?

Some dinosaurs ate meat. These were ferocious creatures that caught and killed other animals for food, just as tigers and sharks do now.

Other dinosaurs were vegetarians. They were large creatures, too, but not so terrifying. They ate grass, and chewed the leaves of small trees or plants, just as elephants and cows do today.

Baby dinosaurs hatched from eggs laid by their mothers, like birds or snakes do.

Some full-grown dinosaurs could run as fast as a horse. But the largest dinosaurs probably moved around more slowly, wandering about with their families in herds, rather like giraffes.

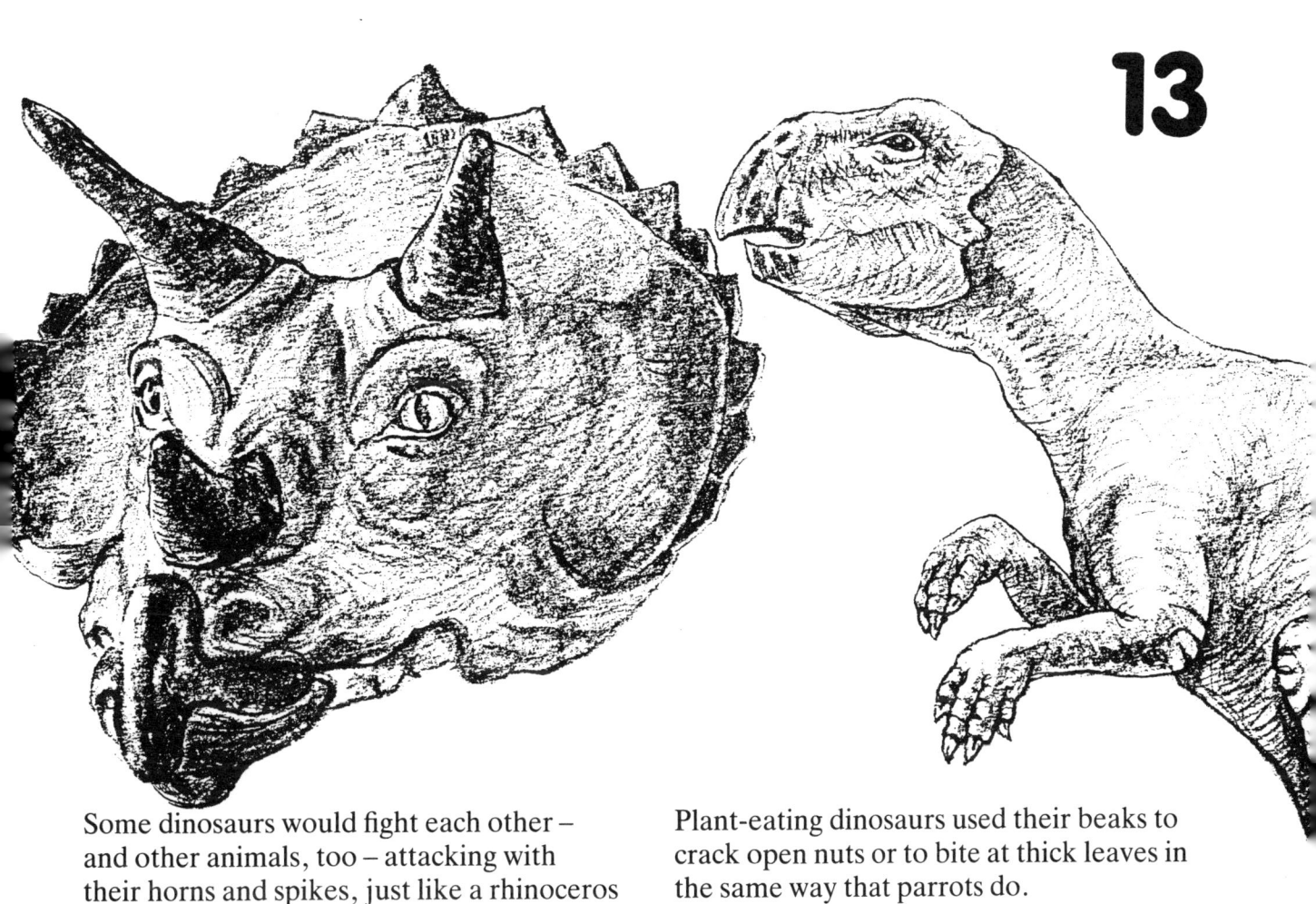

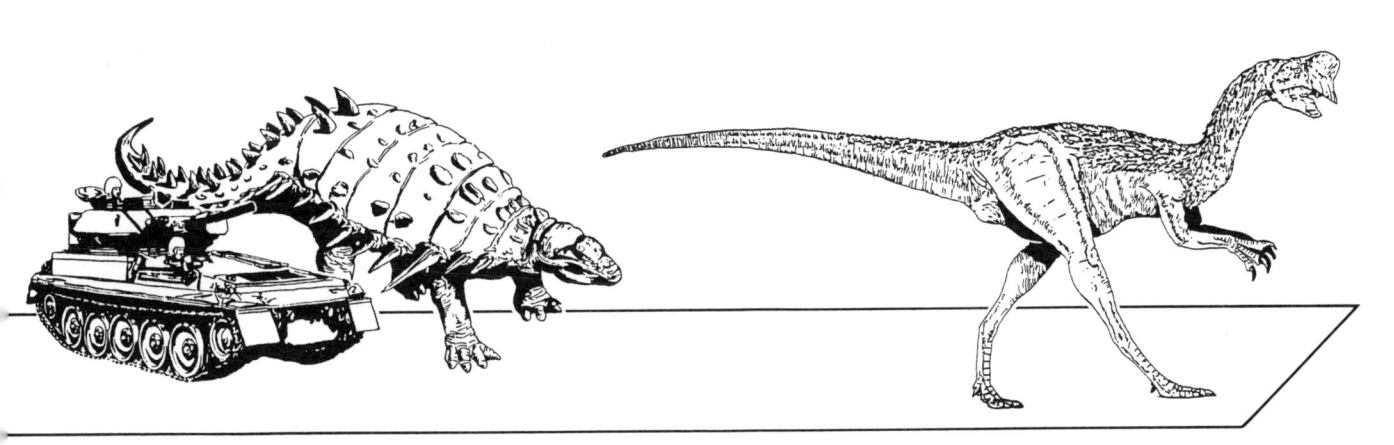

Some dinosaurs would fight each other – and other animals, too – attacking with their horns and spikes, just like a rhinoceros will do.

Plant-eating dinosaurs used their beaks to crack open nuts or to bite at thick leaves in the same way that parrots do.

Some dinosaurs were covered in thick shells which made them almost as strong as a tank. They needed these shells for protection, just as crabs and tortoises do.

Some dinosaurs may have been bright green, yellow or a reddish brown. Others may have been grey. They were probably covered in scales like snakes. But some may have had feathers.

©DIAGRAM

How big were dinosaurs?

Not all dinosaurs were the same size. Some were as big as a house and weighed more than a elephant. Others were almost as small as a pet dog. We know this from bones and footprints that have been found.

Many different types of dinosaur are shown here. Would you rather have been chased by a **Tyrannosaurus** (tie-ran-oh-saw-rus) or a **Velociraptor** (vel-oh-see-rap-tor)? I know which I would prefer to meet on a dark night!

1 **Apatosaurus**
   (a-pat-oh-saw-rus)
2 **Tyrannosaurus**
   (tie-ran-oh-saw-rus)
3 **Stegosaurus**
   (steg-oh-saw-rus)
4 **Velociraptor**
   (vel-oh-see-rap-tor)
5 **Archaeopteryx**
   (ark-ay-op-ter-ricks)
6 **Euoplocephalus**
   (you-op-low-kef-al-us)
7 **Compsognathus**
   (komp-so-nay-thus)
8 **Triceratops**
   (try-ser-a-tops)
9 **Pachycephalosaurus**
   (pak-ee-kef-al-oh-saw-rus)
10 **Parasaurolophus**
   (para-saw-roll-loaf-us)
11 **Quetzalcoatlus**
   (kwet-zal-coat-lus)

15

When and where did dinosaurs live?

Dinosaurs lived all over the world, even near the South Pole. All those millions of years ago, there were only a few great land masses. America was joined to Europe, and there was no ocean between – so you could have walked from where Canada is now all the way to France or Great Britain. The climate was very different then, too.

The **Triassic** (tri-ass-sick) age began 225 million years ago. There were lots of desert areas at this time, and the first dinosaurs lived then. Among them was the **Staurikosaurus** (store-ik-oh-saw-rus) known for its speed.

The **Jurassic** (jaw-rass-sick) age started about 193 million years back. It lasted for more than ten times as long as we humans have existed. During this time, most of the largest dinosaurs wandered the Earth, which

17

Scientists have arranged the story of the past into several different ages lasting millions of years. During each of these, there were different types of dinosaurs roaming about the Earth. You can see some of them here.

was getting warmer and wetter. The long-necked, plant-eating **Brachiosaurus** (brack-ee-oh-saw-rus) was around then, for example. You can find a picture of it on page 25.

The **Cretaceous** (kret-aish-us) age began 136 million years ago. It was the time of the last giant meat-eating dinosaurs like the **Tyrannosaurus** (tie-ran-oh-saw-rus) and the plant-eating horned **Triceratops** (try-ser-a-tops).

©DIAGRAM

Part 2

What sort of paper is it best to draw on? How can you use pencils, chalks, crayons and paints to get different effects? And what about drawing with ink?

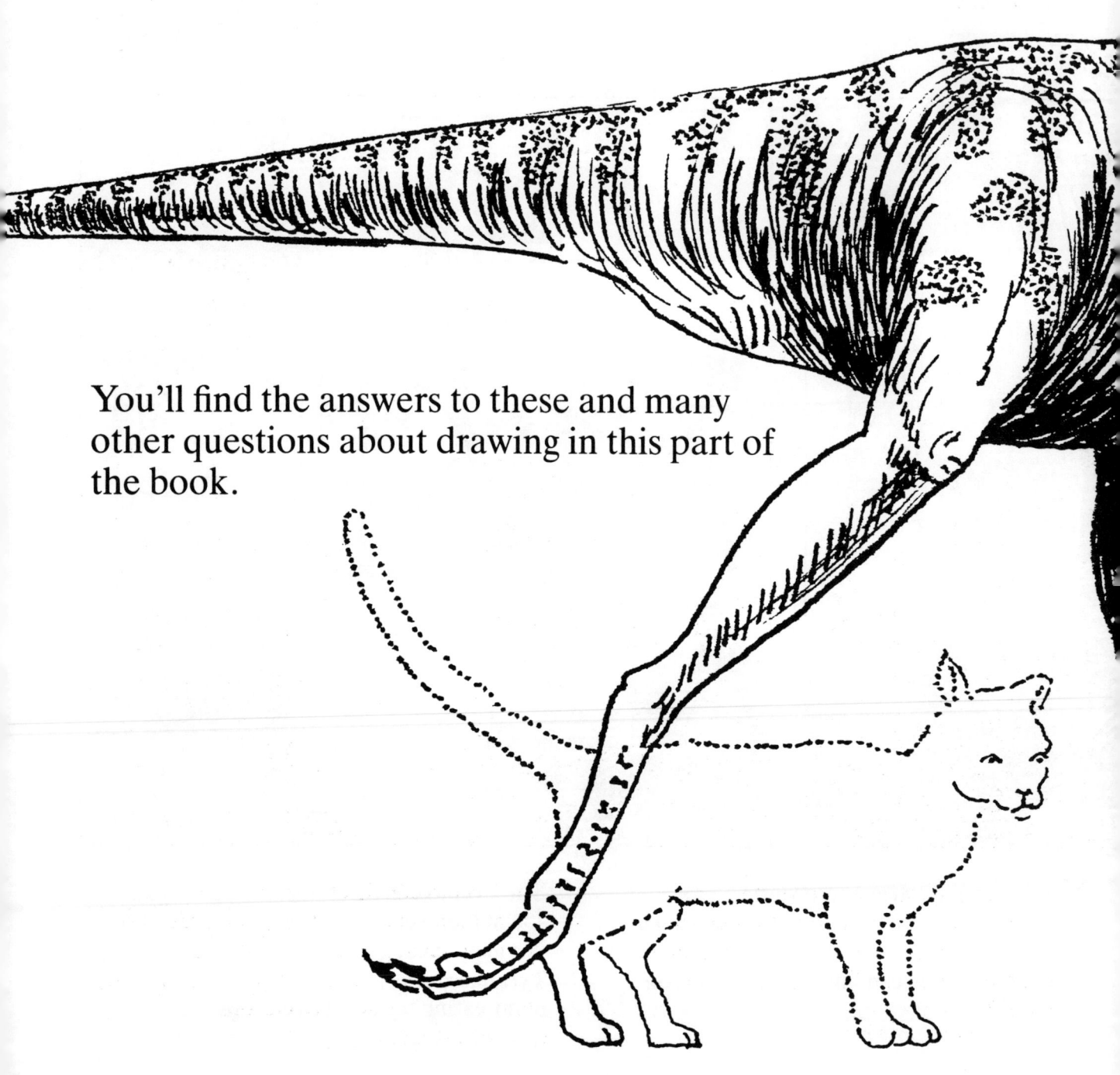

You'll find the answers to these and many other questions about drawing in this part of the book.

GETTING READY TO DRAW 19

This creature is a **Caenagnathus** (ky-nag-nar-thus). About three times as big as a cat, it lived in that part of the world we now call Canada. Mary traced it with a felt-tip pen from a pencil outline. Felt-tips are fun to use. They can produce smooth lines or tiny dots. You can also sometimes flick them like a brush to get an interesting effect. Find out more about them on page 29.

©DIAGRAM

Good places to draw

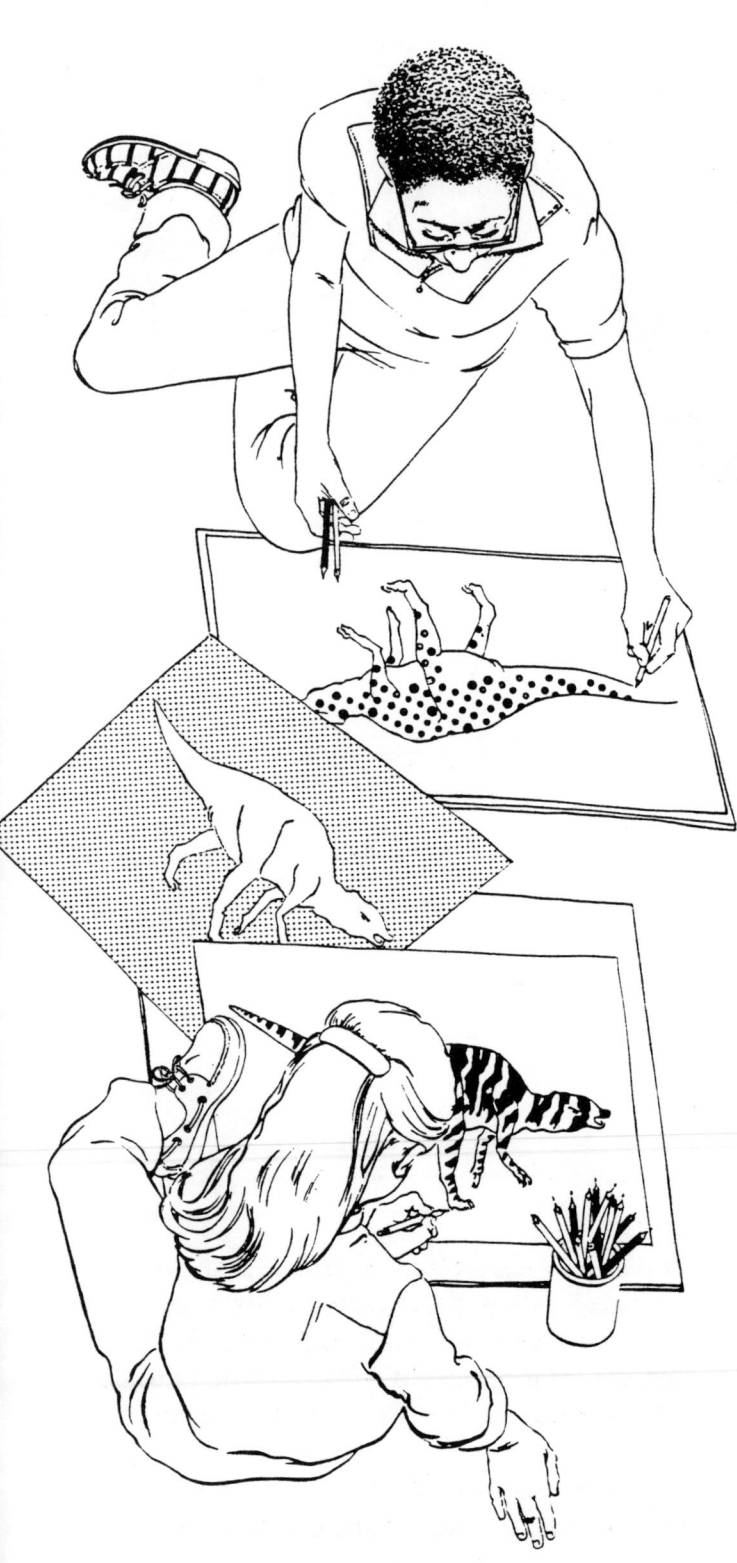

Before you get started, take a little time to choose the space you are going to work in. Get everything ready,.too.

Would you like to spend time drawing with a friend? Or would you prefer to draw on your own? Make up your mind before you begin.

Working on the floor can be fun. It will also give you lots of space so that you can lay out all the pencils, paints, crayons or pens and paper you will be needing. (But make sure that any rug or carpet on the floor is covered with old newspaper or a plastic sheet before you start.) If you work on the floor, you can also stand up from time to time to take a good look at your drawings.

Have a hard surface like a board or a piece of cardboard on which to put the paper you draw on. It will be best, too, if the paper is not so large that you will need to lean on the drawing to reach a far corner.

But working on a table is sometimes a bit easier, as you can get really close to your drawings when you lean forward.

Wherever you choose to work, make sure you have plenty of light. By a window may be best. If you are right-handed, try to sit so that the light from a window or a lamp comes over your left shoulder. If you are left-handed, try to arrange things so that the light comes over your right shoulder.

Reminders!

- Think about what you would like to draw before you start.

- Decide whether you will use a pencil, ballpoint pen, felt-tips, crayons, chalks or paints. Or perhaps ink?

- How large will your drawing be? Plan it so that it will fit your paper.

- Try not to hurry your drawing. You can always come back to it later if someone calls you away.

Which tools for different effects?

These pictures are taken from three different drawings in this book. Can you tell whether they were drawn with chalk, felt-tips, ink, pencils, crayons or paints? Find them in the book to check if you were right. (The pages to turn to are shown by each whole drawing on the right.)

The first picture in each row, going across these two pages, is part of the whole picture at the size it was drawn. The next picture is a detail from it, shown bigger. The third picture shows the whole drawing at a smaller size. Each picture has a very different effect, hasn't it?

Before you start to draw, think about the sort of effect you want. Will you need a lot of dark areas? Would you like to be able to rub out any mistakes? Will you want to show a lot of detail? The next few pages tell you whether you should choose pencils, felt-tips, crayons, paints, ink or a ballpoint pen once you have decided what you want your drawing to look like.

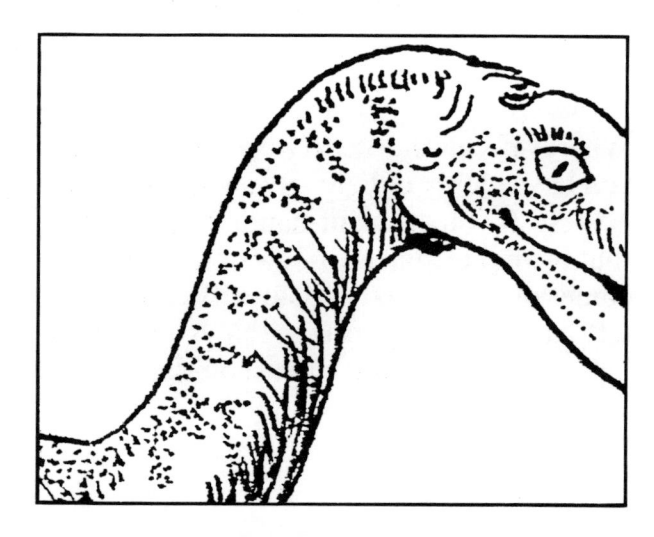

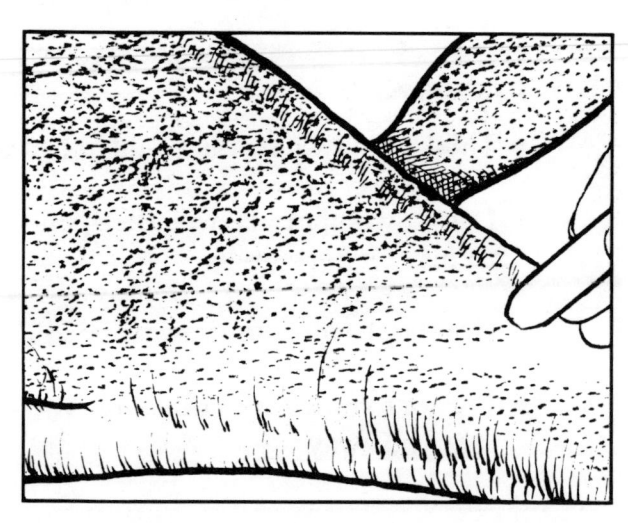

23

Page 77

Pages 18–19

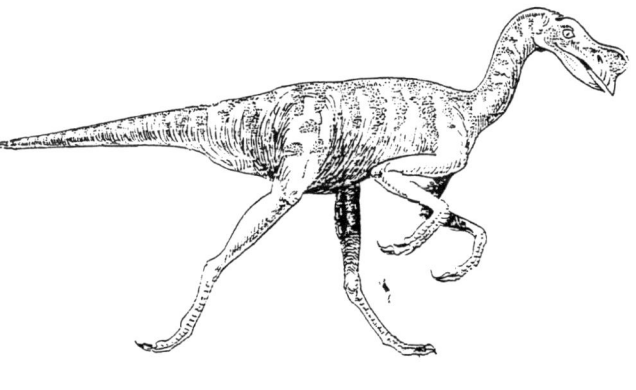

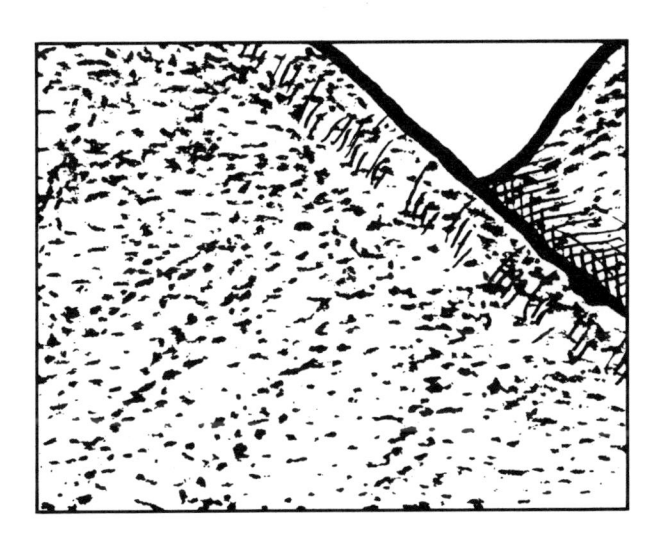

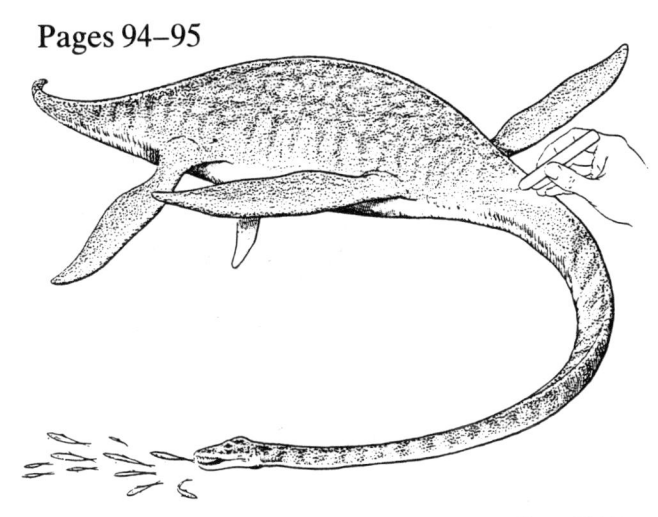

Pages 94–95

© DIAGRAM

Drawing with pencils

Most people like drawing with pencils. They are easy to use and can be rubbed out when you are planning a picture or if you make a mistake.

When you buy a pencil, you'll see it has a grade (a letter and perhaps a number, too) on the side. If you would like to make dark, smudgy lines, look for grades B or 2B. These are soft. For fine, hard lines, use a pencil with an H or 2H grade.

A soft pencil is by far the best for planning a drawing as a B or 2B pencil is easy to rub out. You can, of course, get pencils in lots of different shades – with red, blue, green, orange, yellow, brown or purple leads, for example.

Always keep your pencils sharpened. There should be just enough lead showing so that the point will not snap when you work. Rubbing the side of your pencil lead across a sheet of sandpaper will give it a good sharp point.

Pencils work best on paper that has a rough surface. Store them in a box, or keep them in a jar with their points upward.

This is a pencil drawing of a **Brachiosaurus** (brack-ee-oh-saw-rus) from Africa. Ryozo, who drew it, used a soft pencil (2B) to shade in the grey areas. But he then used a very sharp 2H pencil to draw in details like the eye and the toes.

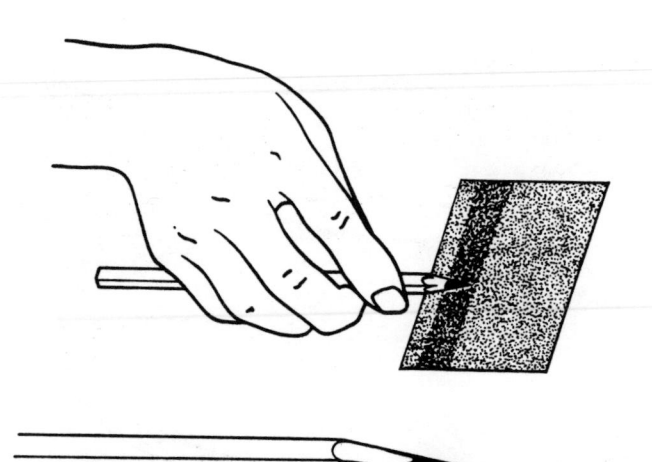

25

Drawing with chalks and crayons

There are several different sorts of chalks and crayons. All of them will give your drawings lots of action, as you can see in the picture of a dinosaur fight shown here. But they may smudge easily if you are not careful. Use paper with a rough surface for the best results.

This is a chalk and charcoal drawing by Ryozo of a **Deinonychus** (die-no-nike-us) from North America fighting a **Tenontosaurus** (ten-on-toe-saw-rus). The chalks were used to give the picture lots of light and dark areas. Details in the heads and the claws were picked out in charcoal.

1 **Pastel sticks** come in a large number of shades and are covered in paper so that your hands don't get grubby when you pick them up.

2 **Pastel pencils** work a bit like lead pencils but it is difficult to keep them sharp. This means that they are better for shading in than drawing.

3 **Chalks** give interesting textures but you cannot sharpen them.

4 **Charcoal sticks** are often used by artists and are always black.

5 **Wax crayons** also come in lots of shades and different thicknesses. They are good for covering large areas but are often hard to rub out.

27

While you are drawing with chalks, crayons or charcoal, remember to rest your hand on a spare piece of paper so that you do not smudge your picture.

©DIAGRAM

Drawing with pens

Marks made with any sort of ink do not rub out. This means that if you decide to draw with ink, you need to do a pencil outline or sketch first before you begin your final picture. You can, of course, also trace using ink.

Ink will not give you a chance to shade like you can with a pencil or chalk. So if you use a pen to do your drawing, you will have to build up darker areas in your picture with lots of dots or criss-cross lines.

Remember to keep the tops on your felt-tip pens when you are not using them or the ink may dry up.

Try to keep ink off your hands while you are drawing or you may get blotches and fingermarks all over your drawings. Take care not to spill the ink, too, if you are using a fountain pen or dip pen. And try not to get it on your clothes. It is sometimes difficult to wash out.

Philip drew this head of a **Megalosaurus** (meg-a-low-saw-rus) using three types of pen, as you can see.

Fountain pens and dip pens
Dip pens and fountain pens (which often come with cartridges so that you do not need a bottle of ink) can be bought with nibs of different widths. This means that some will make thinner lines when you draw than others. Many professional artists prefer dip pens, however. This is because you can also change the thickness of a line by using a different amount of ink.

The sort of lines you can make with a fountain pen or dip pen seem more alive and exciting than those you can make with felt-tips or a ballpoint. Try them all out, if you can, and see the difference for yourself.

Ballpoint pens
They tend to smudge, so work carefully just as you would with chalks. (Turn back to pages 26–27 for information about these.) It is difficult to shade large areas with a ballpoint, and you will only get lines of the same thickness.

Felt-tips
These are popular for drawing and come with differently shaped tips. Some make fine lines, and some which are chunky are better for shading. They are also useful for filling in large areas of the background to your picture. (Let's hope Philip didn't forget to put that top back on.)

Using brushes

If you use a brush, you can water down your paint or ink to get lighter shades.
You can give soft edges to your drawings, too, using watered-down paints.

Brushes come in different thicknesses. Larger ones are good for filling in bigger areas. Finer ones are better for drawing lines. The very best brushes are made from sable or squirrel hair, but cheaper ones can be very good, too.

31

Use strong paper when you work with a brush. If you paint on very thin paper, your drawing may curl up.

As you paint, start with lighter tones and build them up into darker areas slowly. Wait until large areas are dry. Then add detail with a pen or a pencil.

Use your brushes gently. Don't put too much paint on them or you may get blotches everywhere.

Wash all your brushes after you have used them and store them in a jar so that the brush ends point upward. This will prevent you from damaging them.

©DIAGRAM

Making textures

Find a piece of sandpaper and run your hand over it. Rough, isn't it? Now try to find a piece of silk and run your hand over that. You can feel the difference, can't you? The sandpaper and the silk look very different and they also have a different sort of texture when you feel them.

Giving the effect of texture to your drawings, so that you can almost feel what it would be like to stroke a dinosaur, is easier than it seems. There are lots of ways to do it.

Enjoy experimenting with texture! But I suggest you try out everything on a piece of scrap paper first before you give texture to your final drawing.

Smudge it!
If you work on strong paper with pencils or chalks, you can rub or smudge parts of your drawing with a finger or using a tissue – not by accident but on purpose – to get a soft effect.

Rub it!
If you draw on thin paper, after you have finished your outline, place it over a rough surface (sandpaper, a plank of wood or some fabric) and then rub crayon across the area you want to cover. This will give you a texture like the sandpaper, wood or fabric that you put underneath the paper. Turn to page 95 if you would like to see a **Plesiosaur** (ples-ee-oh-saw) drawn with lots of texture to its body.

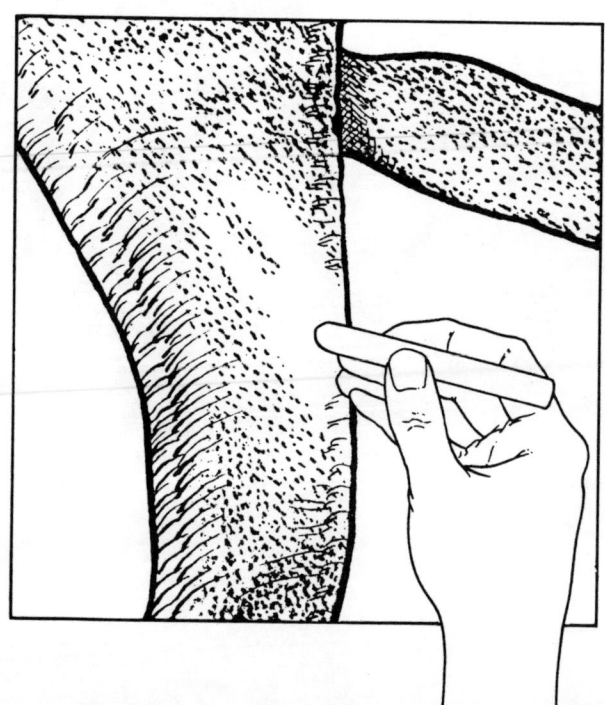

33

Scrape it!
You can sometimes scrape off parts of a drawing if you have worked with paint or ink on very strong paper. This will give the effect of a creature with very rough skin. You can use a nail file for this.

Dab it!
If you work with a pen and ink, you can carefully dab the edges of your drawing with a wet tissue to give a softer effect. But be sure to work with strong paper if you would like to try this out, or the wet tissue may make a hole in it. I made the dabs on the drawing on page 135 with a wet finger.

Splatter it!
This is fun! When you have finished drawing a dinosaur outline, cut it out and put it on some old newspaper. Find an old toothbrush that you are sure no one wants anymore. Dip the brush into ink or paint and splatter a spray at the drawing, flicking off the paint with a small stick. (It is best to wear a smock when you do this.)

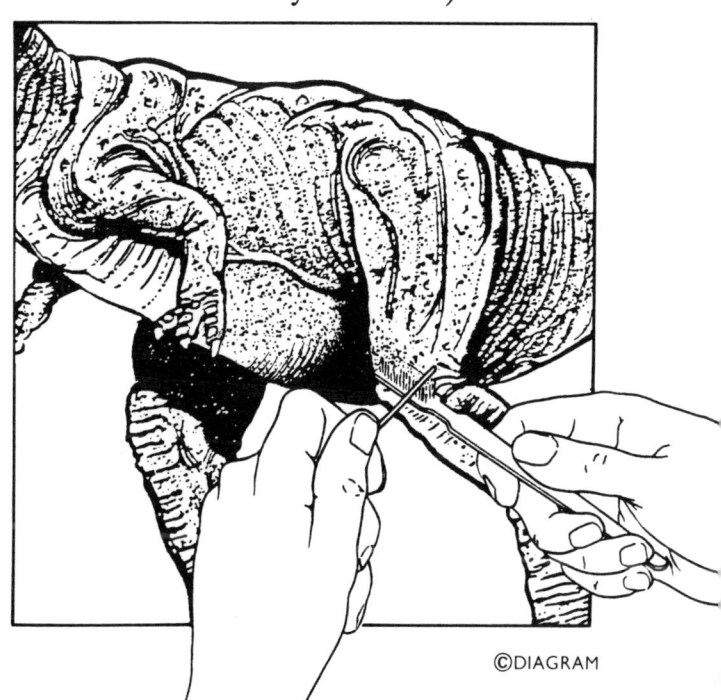

©DIAGRAM

Making special effects

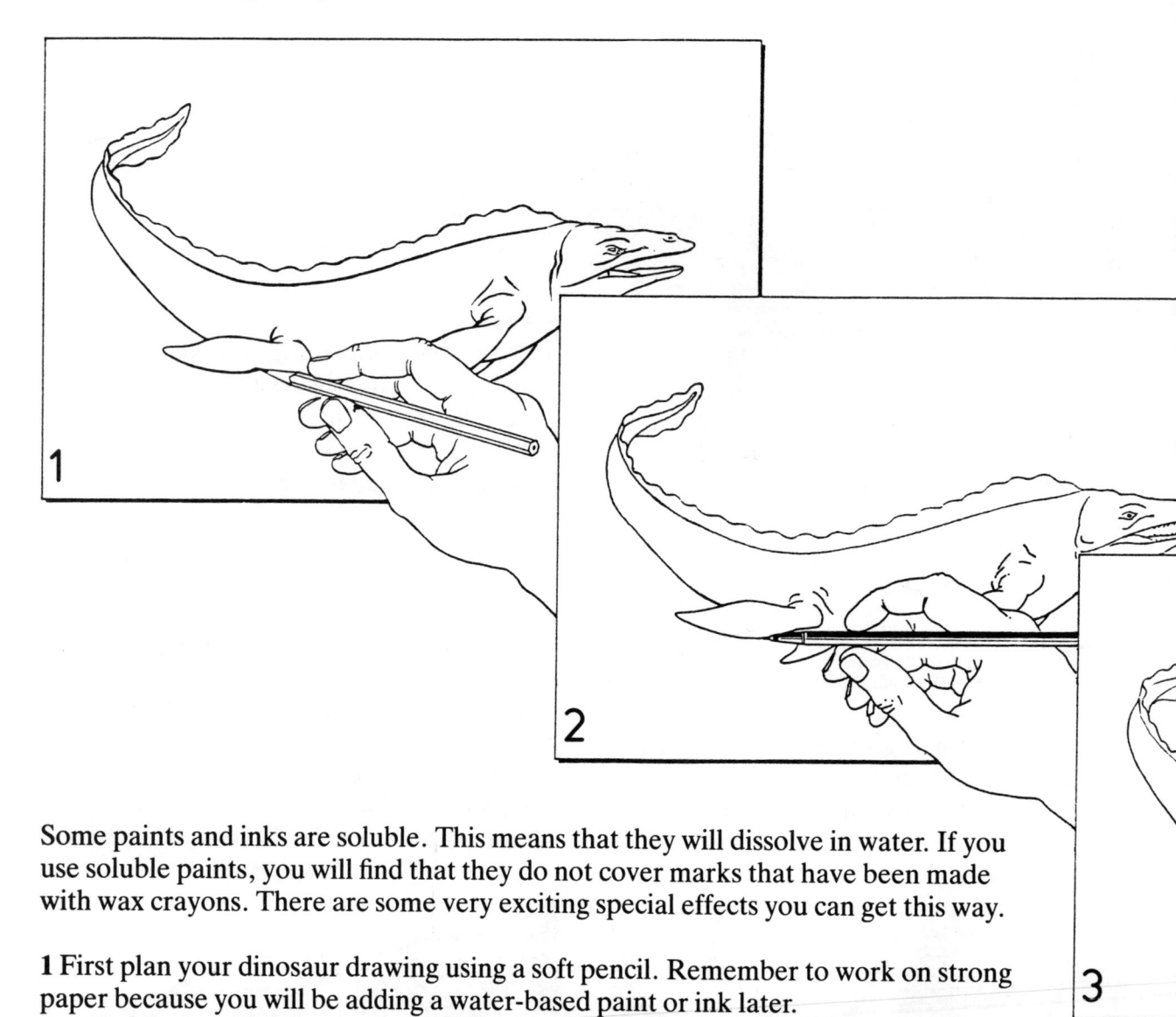

Some paints and inks are soluble. This means that they will dissolve in water. If you use soluble paints, you will find that they do not cover marks that have been made with wax crayons. There are some very exciting special effects you can get this way.

1 First plan your dinosaur drawing using a soft pencil. Remember to work on strong paper because you will be adding a water-based paint or ink later.

2 Next put in the detail and dark areas with a hard pencil, ballpoint pen or felt-tip.

3 Now rub a white, yellow, pink or pale green wax crayon over those areas you would like to keep light in your drawing.

4 Paint over the dark tones in your dinosaur drawing. Then try to paint over the areas covered with wax crayon. You should find that they do not take the paint. The result is that there will be areas in your picture that have different textures.

The detail at the top of the next page shows the effect you can get if you use water-based paints and wax crayon in this way. You can see the whole drawing on page 97.

35

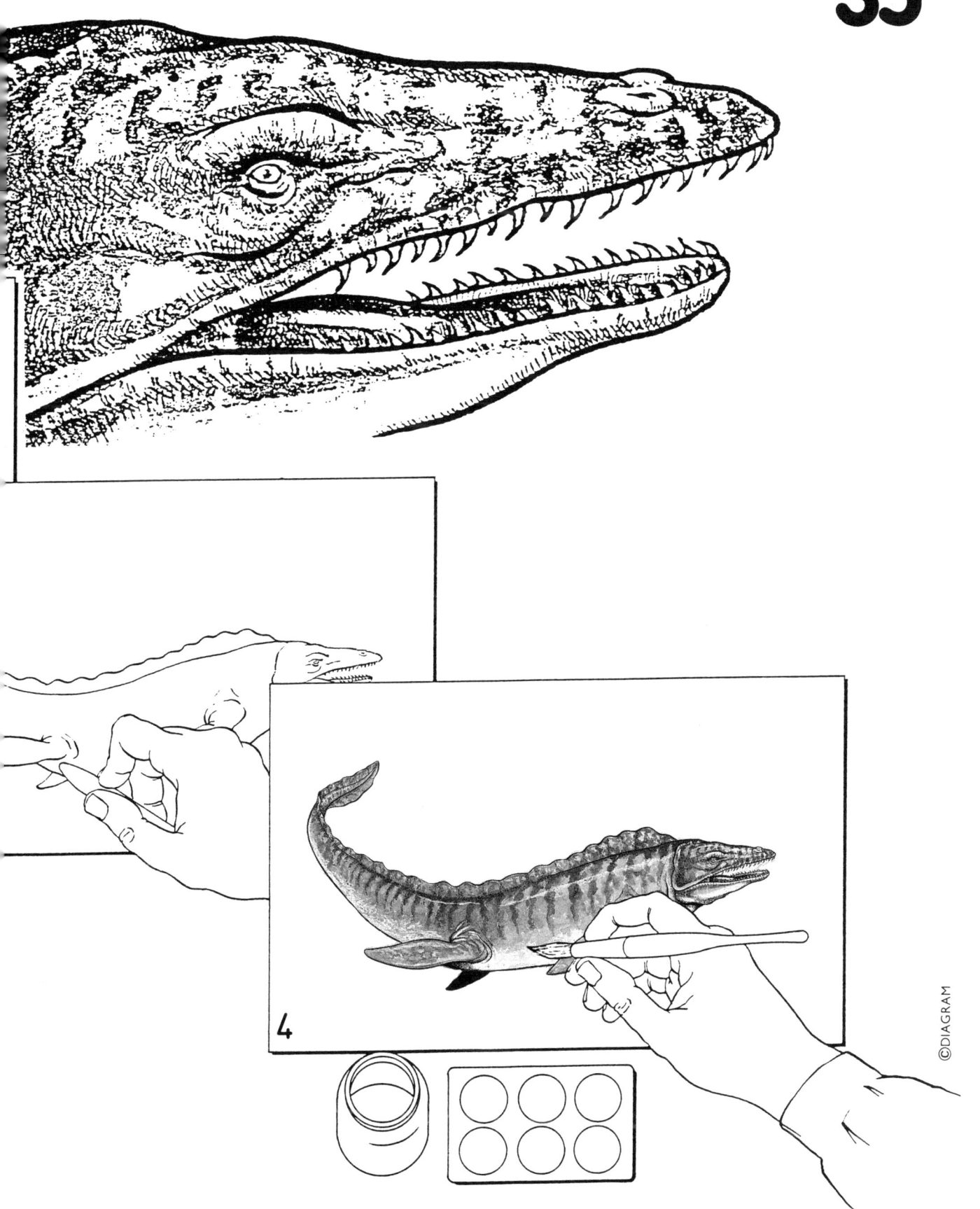

Choosing paper

The sort of paper you should use depends on whether you are working with a pencil, crayons, chalks, inks or paint. If you use very thin paper, for instance, you cannot work with paints as the paper may curl up.

If you use thick paper, you cannot trace a drawing. So you will need to plan your picture carefully. Or you could perhaps transfer a tracing on to a thick paper, using the method you will find on page 39.

Tracing paper
It is always useful to have some thin paper that you can see through. This will be helpful because you can learn a lot by tracing pictures of dinosaurs from books. You can also trace drawings you have already made.

Follow very carefully the method described on page 39 if you would like to discover the secret of how to transfer a tracing onto a piece of thick paper.

Once you have traced an outline, you can also trace some of the picture's detail or you may prefer to add your own. But remember that, when you trace, you should not press too hard or you may spoil the picture you are copying.

Looking after your paper
A lot of people throw away good paper that you might use for drawing. If someone in your family does this, see if you can rescue it. Even small pieces are useful for rough sketches. Save them for the next time you draw.

Keep all your drawing paper flat if you can. But if it comes in a roll, simply roll it back the other way to stop it curling up again.

Always work with clean hands. This will help you avoid dirty fingermarks all over your work.

Points to remember about paper
- Tracing paper is very useful if you want to copy drawings from books. You can also use it to transfer drawings on to cardboard or thick paper. But you cannot use a paintbrush on tracing paper very well.

- Smooth paper is usually good for felt-tips and soft pencils. But it is not very strong, so it is best not to use water-paints on this sort of paper.

- Some papers, which you can buy in an art shop, come in lots of different shades other than white, and will usually take paint.

- Strong drawing paper is also sold in art shops, and will usually have a rough surface. This means it is good for pencils, inks, chalks and paints.

- The thickness of a paper is called its weight. So when you buy paper you can ask for a heavyweight or lightweight sort.

Drawing pads
You can buy paper in single sheets at an art shop. But you can also buy drawing pads. These are often a good idea as it means you can keep all your pictures in one place. You could also label a drawing pad on the front cover with the title *My Dinosaur Sketchbook*, and add your name.

Doing a tracing

Sometimes it can help to trace an outline of a dinosaur from a book. You can then add your own shading.

Choose a picture with a bold shape so that you do not get muddled about which lines to follow on the tracing paper. A pencil will usually be best for tracing, but you can also use a ballpoint or a felt-tip.

You can trace any picture in this book. To help you start, here is a picture of two dinosaurs in combat for you to trace. It shows a **Tyrannosaurus** (tie-ran-oh-saw-rus) fighting a **Corythosaurus** (ko-rith-oh-saw-rus). Do you know which is which?

If you would like to transfer a tracing onto a thick piece of paper or cardboard, you can easily do this using the following method. Try it out on the drawing opposite of a **Dimetrodon** (di-met-roh-don) which you will also find at a much larger size on page 133.

First cover the picture with clear tracing paper, and fix it to the page with the sort of tape that peels off without leaving a mark. This is usually called masking tape. Do not use ordinary sticky tape – it will damage the book.

Using a sharp, soft pencil (grade B), draw round the main shape. You can also trace any of the details you think it may be hard to copy later, if you like.

Now remove the tracing paper. Turn it over, and rub with a soft pencil or chalk over the lines that show through to the back of the tracing paper. Turn the tracing paper back again to its right side. Now put it on a piece of plain paper or cardboard. This time, use a hard pencil (2H) with a sharp point and go over all the lines firmly but not too hard.

When you take the tracing paper away, you should find a shadow of the drawing on the paper or cardboard. You can use these ghost lines as part of your own drawing.

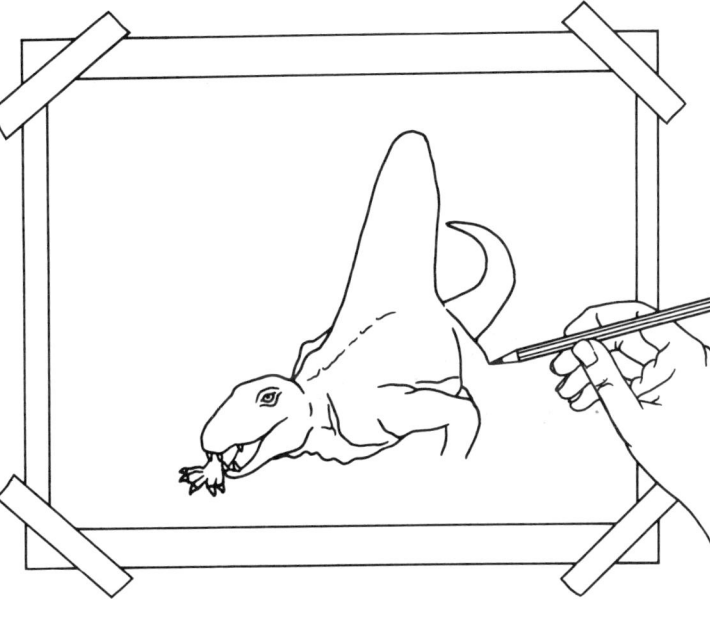

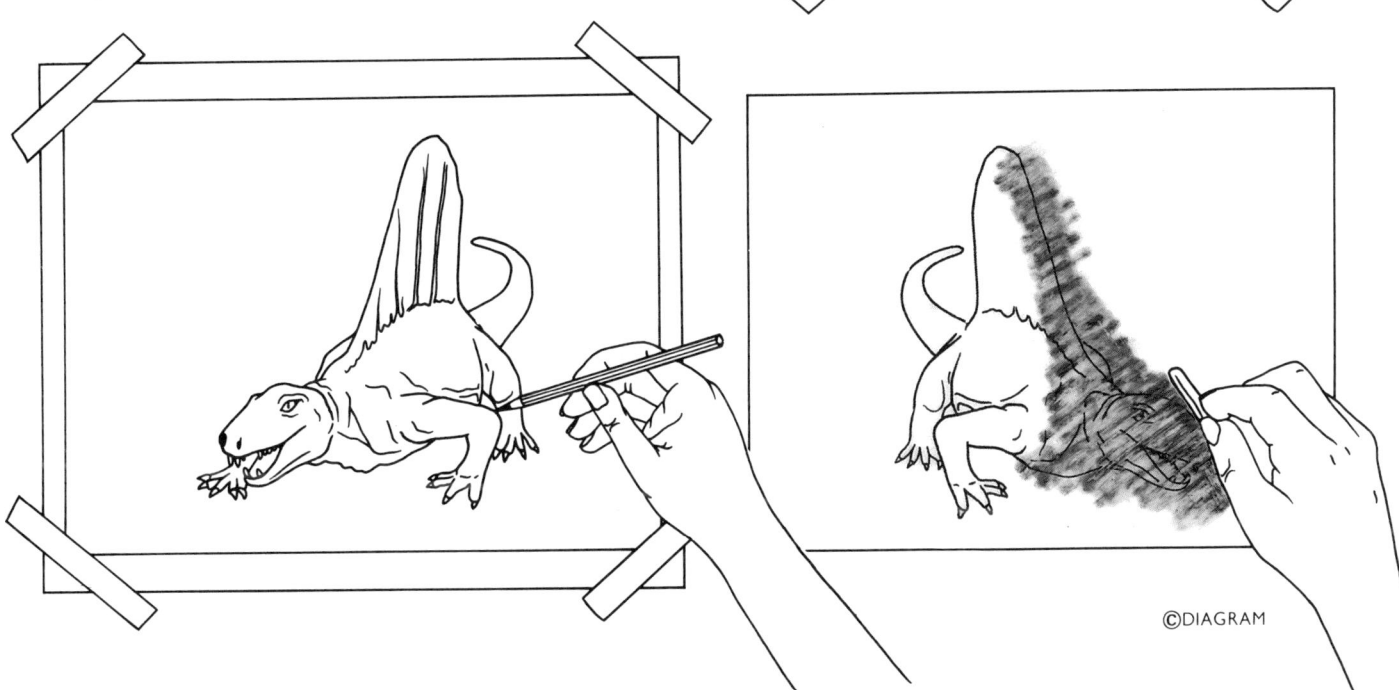

Copying drawings

Copying drawings will give you lots of ideas for your own pictures. Try hard to get the shapes and tones right, or your copy will not look like the original. Of course, if you use a pencil and the original was drawn in ink, the two will be very different. One drawing will look softer than the other. Here are some useful tips to help you master the art of copying.

Plan your drawing
Using a soft pencil, draw the basic shape first before you try to copy any detail.

Keep checking your drawing
When you are copying, keep looking back at the original drawing to check that you are putting everything in the right place. Check where the legs start, and where the eyes are, for example.

Look at the drawing on the left of this page. I have started to copy it, as you can see. First of all, I measured the length of the dinosaur's head, and then the space between its eye and front claws, using a ruler. I also checked that the position of the eye was almost directly above the claws.

Check for size, too
In the original drawing, the dinosaur's eye is the same size as one of its claws. I have drawn them side by side so that you can see this clearly. When you are copying, you need to keep checking the size of details like this.

Turn to page 51 or page 53 if you would like to try copying a few simple dinosaur shapes. Once you find it quite easy, you might like to try copying this wonderful **Stegosaurus** (steg-oh-saw-rus) from Colorado USA. It had a brain the size of a walnut but looked terrifying. Notice how short its front legs were, and the spikes on its tail, too.

Making drawings bigger

It is easy to change the size of your drawing or any picture you are copying from a book by using squares.

First turn the drawing you would like to enlarge upside down so that the top of the picture is now at the bottom. This will help you to concentrate when you copy the outline. Then trace the drawing using a pencil.

Next draw squares over your tracing, as shown, using a ruler for straight lines. Make sure all the lines are the same distance apart. First draw them down your tracing paper and then across.

Now take a larger sheet of paper and again draw squares. But this time make the squares larger than those on the tracing paper. Take care that you draw the same number of squares. If there are 24 squares on your tracing paper, there must be 24 larger squares on the larger piece of paper.

Now copy the tracing onto the other sheet of paper, carefully matching what is in each square. For example, the third square from the left at the top of the tracing paper should match the third square from the left at the top of your drawing paper.

Watch where the lines of the picture cross each square on the tracing paper. Make them cross at exactly the same point on the larger squares of the drawing paper.

You should soon have a larger copy of the original outline.

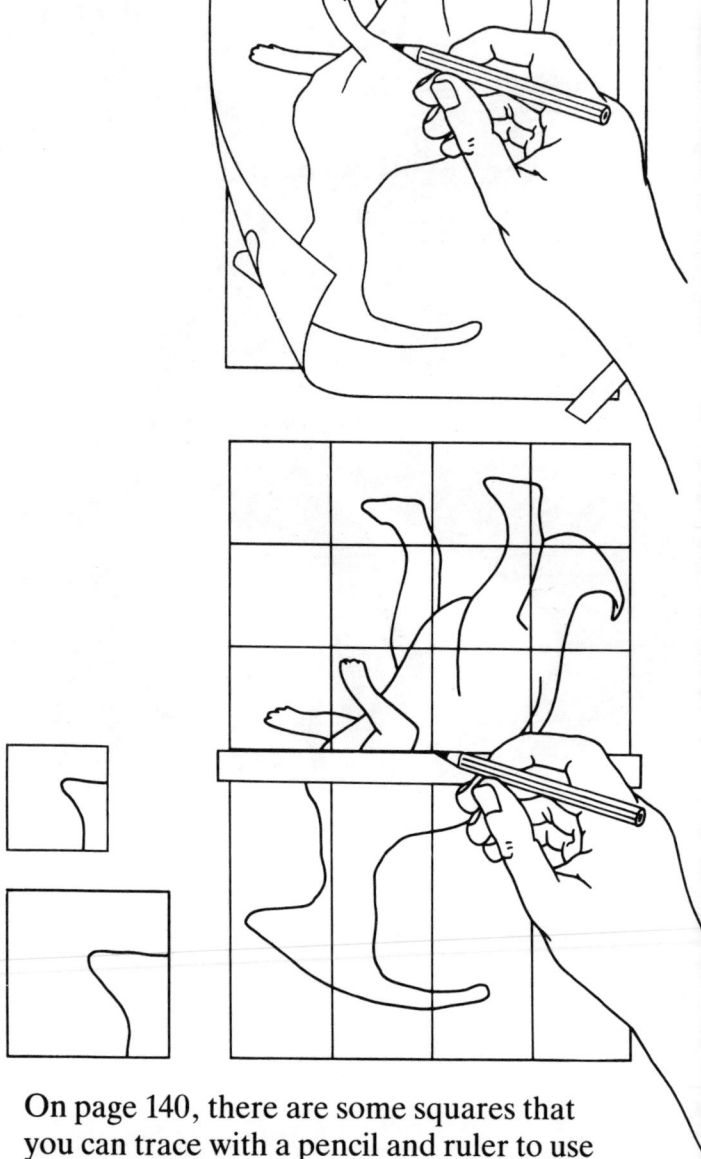

On page 140, there are some squares that you can trace with a pencil and ruler to use for enlarging in this way. Using this tracing of squares, copy the shapes inside the boxes on page 43. When you have finished, turn your tracing paper upside down. Can you recognize which creatures you have drawn? Turn to page 107 and page 121 to find out.

43

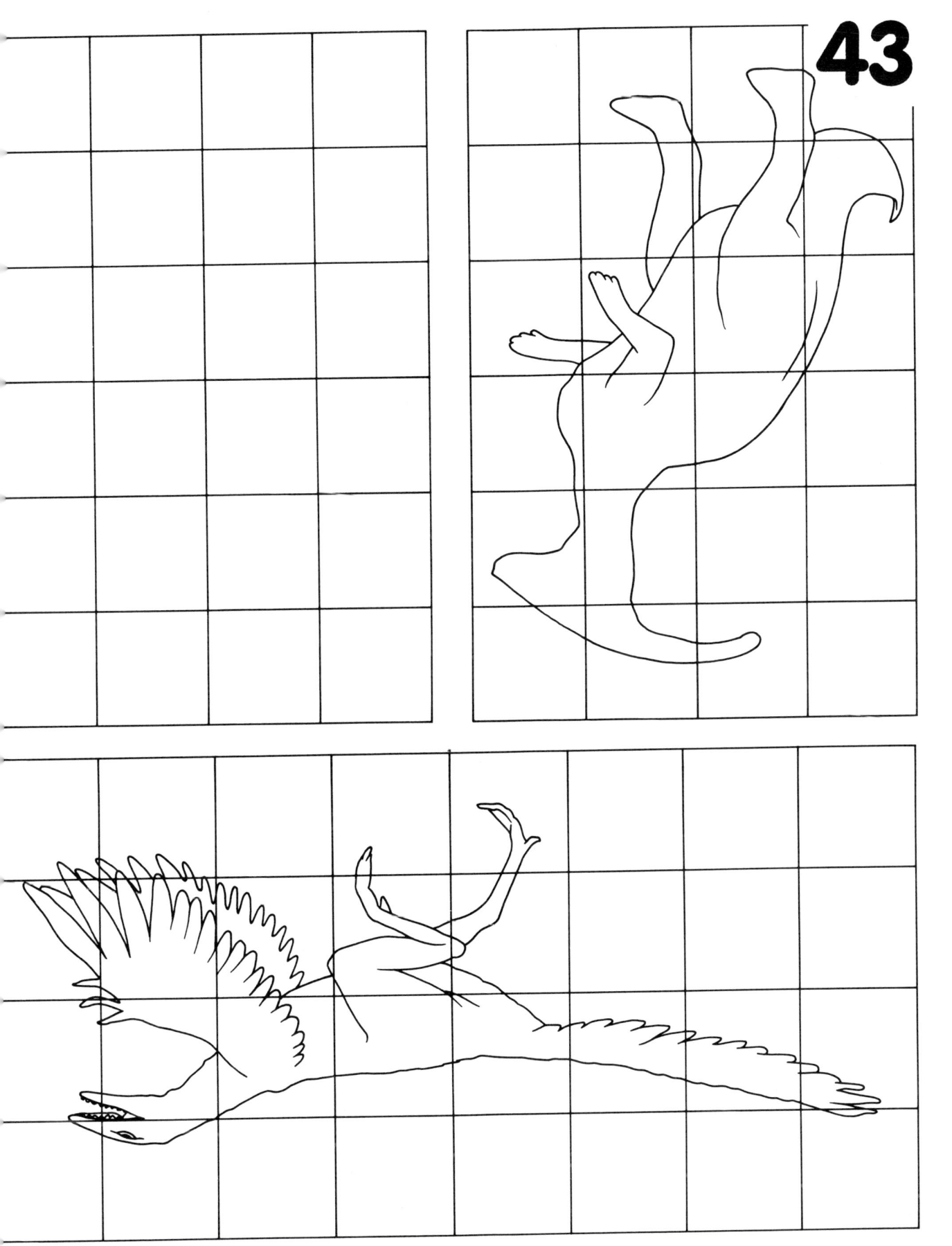

Using your drawings

There are lots of interesting things you can do with your drawings of dinosaurs when you have finished them. So try to think about how you would like to use your pictures before you start. Here are some ideas to add to your own.

Try cutting out simple dinosaur shapes and making them into mobiles to hang up with thread or some wire from the ceiling. It will be best to draw on cardboard rather than paper for this.

You can make a frieze by drawing a row of all different kinds of dinosaurs along a roll of paper. You could then put up the frieze on the wall of your room.

You can also make very detailed drawings of dinosaurs to display on the wall. Don't forget to sign them when you have finished and perhaps put the date, too. If they are really good, you could ask if you can have them framed.

Dinosaur cards are fun to make for birthdays or Christmas. If you are sending out party invitations, these could have a dinosaur theme, too. There could either be a drawing on one sheet of paper with the message underneath; or you can make a folded card with a picture on the front and a written message inside. Make sure you have envelopes of the right size before you begin.

You could even make your own comics with different dinosaur characters that have all sorts of adventures which your friends would enjoy reading. Give the comic a name like *Dinosaur Weekly* or *Dinosaur Fun,* for instance.

Perhaps keep a scrapbook and put all your drawings in it, as well as any pictures of dinosaurs that you have cut out from newspapers and magazines, and museum postcards if you have some.

Visit the library and bookshops to find out all you can about how the dinosaurs you have drawn lived. If you get enough information, you could make your own illustrated dinosaur guide.

Part 3

In this part of the book you will find out how to start drawing dinosaurs by using very simple shapes. The **Dryptosaurus** (drip-toe-saw-rus) opposite can be drawn in various ways.

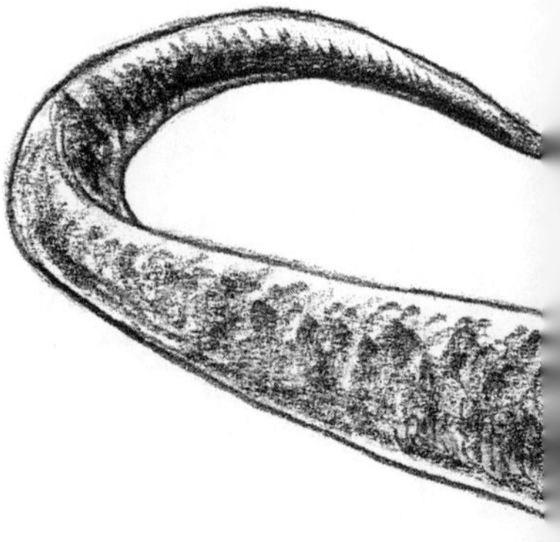

1 You can begin by thinking of the head body and legs as circles, triangles and ovals, for instance.

2 Then you could join them up to make a dinosaur silhouette.

3 You can also add skin texture.

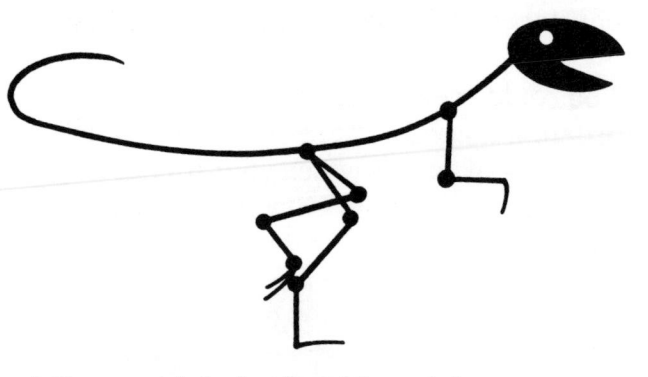

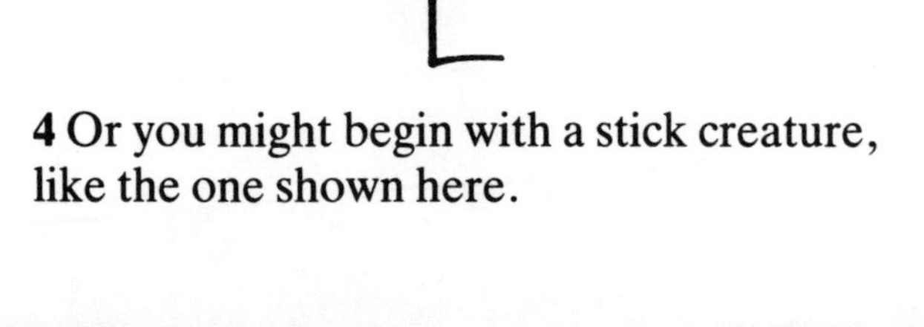

When you have read the next 16 pages, try drawing the **Spinosaurus** (spine-oh-saw-rus) on page 85 as a stick figure, as a silhouette, with textured skin, and with a tin-can body, before you work on a detailed picture.

4 Or you might begin with a stick creature, like the one shown here.

DRAWING DINOSAURS IS EASY!

47

This **Dryptosaurus** (drip-toe-saw-rus) was drawn by Ryozo, using a soft pencil. It was a cousin of the **Sarcosaurus** (sark-oh-saw-rus) on page 89.

5 You could also draw a skeleton. The bones of a dinosaur's skeleton moved just like ours when we jump or turn round. So think about the position of a dinosaur's bones if you draw it reaching up or running.

6 Remember that dinosaurs – like all other creatures – were not flat like a piece of paper but solid and with depth, like a coffee pot. Thinking of a dinosaur as a tin-can creature will help your drawings look more lifelike.

©DIAGRAM

Join the dots

49

Here are four dinosaur outlines, made up from dots. Get some tracing paper, trace the dot rows and then join them up. Now copy the outlines. It is really quite easy to draw a dinosaur shape, isn't it?

©DIAGRAM

Simple shapes

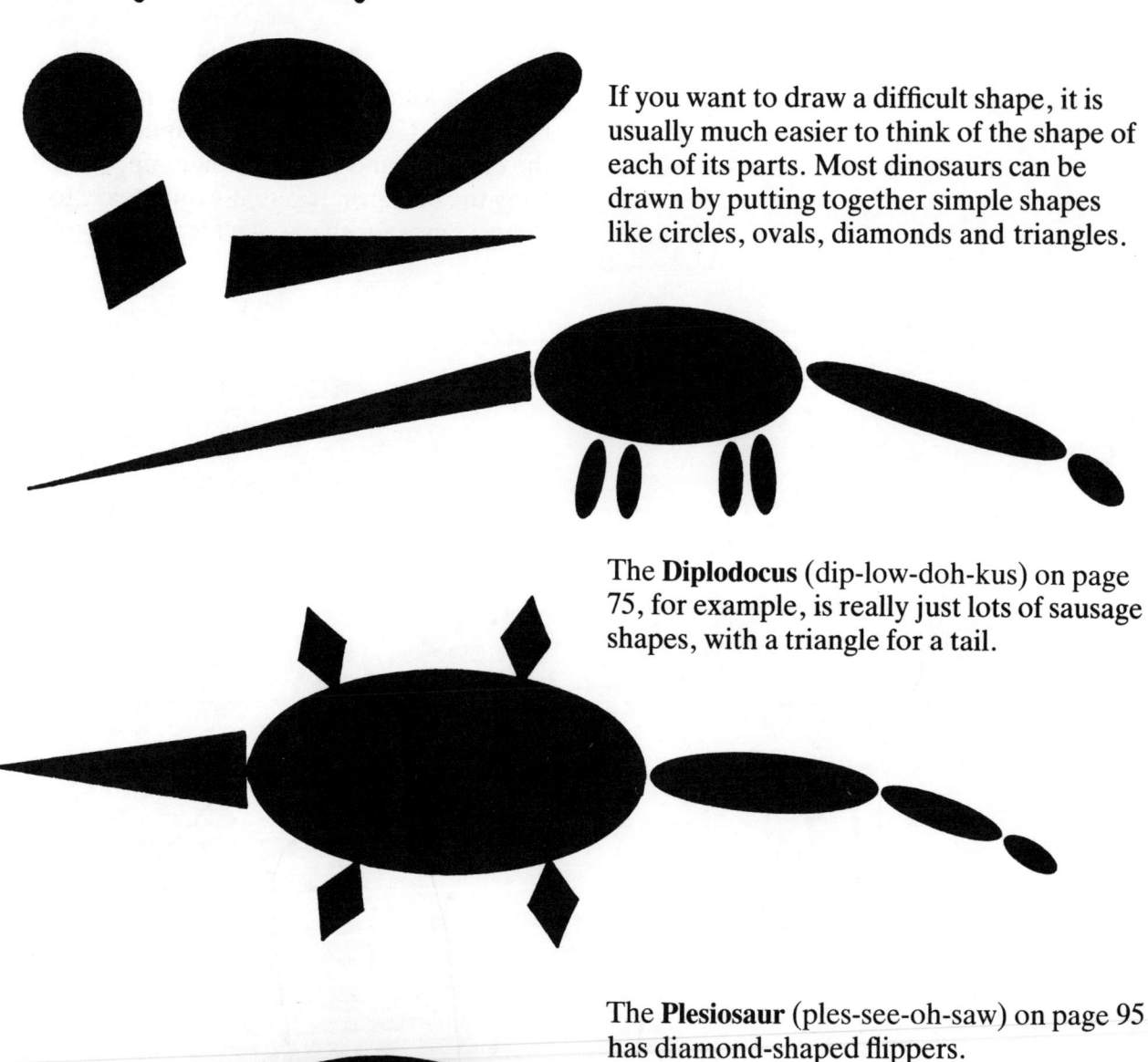

If you want to draw a difficult shape, it is usually much easier to think of the shape of each of its parts. Most dinosaurs can be drawn by putting together simple shapes like circles, ovals, diamonds and triangles.

The **Diplodocus** (dip-low-doh-kus) on page 75, for example, is really just lots of sausage shapes, with a triangle for a tail.

The **Plesiosaur** (ples-see-oh-saw) on page 95 has diamond-shaped flippers.

The **Megatherium** (meg-a-there-ee-um) on page 77 has a body like a big egg, a triangle for a tail and ovals for legs and its head.

The **Torosaurus** (tor-oh-saw-rus) on page 83 has a large protective cape on its shoulders, which can be drawn first of all as a triangle.

The **Mammuthus Primigenius** (mam-oo-thus pree-me-jean-ee-us) on page 81 has an oval body that slopes upwards to a small head like a circle. The front legs are like long sausages, and the back ones are shorter.

The **Dromiceiomimus** (drom-mick-eye-oh-meem-us) on page 87 is made up from small rounded shapes.

The **Dimetrodon** (di-met-roh-don) on page 133 has a fin which is the shape of half a circle.

The **Stegosaurus** (steg-oh-saw-rus) on page 103 has diamond shapes all the way down its back, an oval body, a triangle for a tail, an oval for its head and sausages for its legs.

©DIAGRAM

Dinosaur silhouettes

It is often easiest to draw a dinosaur from the side. When you start your picture, forget about the detail but look carefully at the basic shape of each type of creature and sketch its outline.

You can trace the outline to help you with this, and then fill in the body using a felt-tip or crayons to make a silhouette like those shown.

Flip through the book and see if you can find out the names of each of the dinosaurs drawn here.

The small outlines by the side of each dinosaur will show you how big each was when compared with a man, a mouse or a cat.

53

Skin, feathers and shells

Nobody is sure whether dinosaurs had dark or light skin. Only their bones have survived. Some may have been grey like elephants. Others may have been red, blue, green or yellow, like some snakes and lizards. Others may have had very dark tops and light bellies, like frogs. Some may have had spots or stripes. Others may have had long hair, feathers or a shell.

Use your imagination when it comes to drawing a dinosaur's skin. There are lots of possibilities, and lots of exciting methods to use to create texture.

This is an **Avimimus** (av-ee-meem-us) and it may have had feathers.

55

To show you what a **Saurolophus** (saw-roh-loaf-us) would look like with different markings, for instance, Darren has drawn it with a dark top and a light belly, with spots, stripes and with a rough skin.

Trace the outline, and then use chalks, felt-tips or crayons to make your own skin markings. You can also put all sorts of markings on the skin of other dinosaurs you draw.

©DIAGRAM

Moving dinosaurs

When we move, the various parts of our bodies stay the same shape. But as we bend our arms and knees when running or walking, the shape of our whole body changes. This is true of all animals – dinosaurs, too.

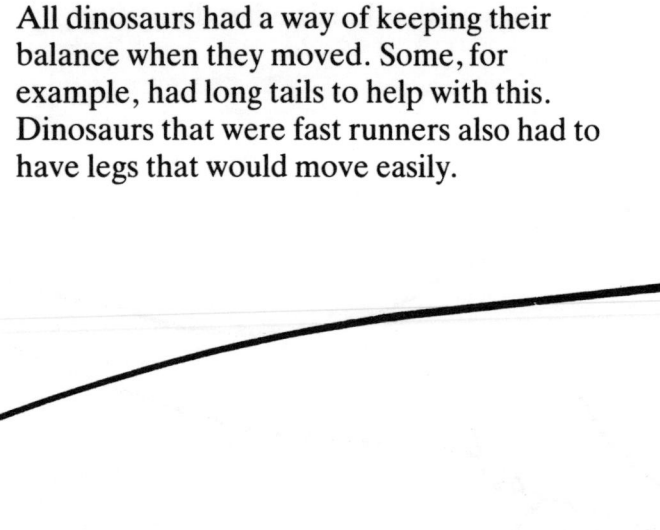

All dinosaurs had a way of keeping their balance when they moved. Some, for example, had long tails to help with this. Dinosaurs that were fast runners also had to have legs that would move easily.

The **Dromiceiomimus** (droh-mick-eye-oh-meem-mus) on page 87 had a great tail and long back legs to help it run like the wind.

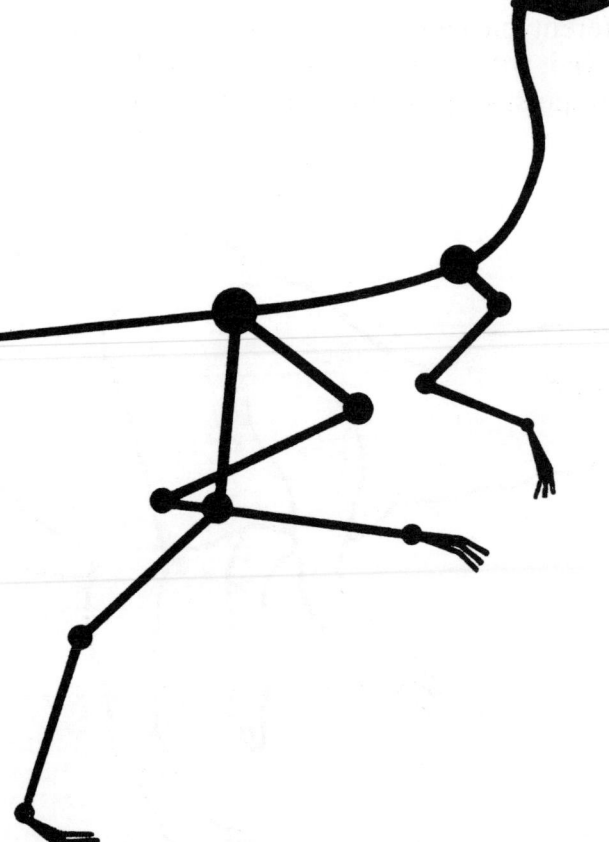

57

If you had X-ray eyes, you would be able to see the skeletons of all your friends. People have various points in their bodies where they can bend – elbows, shoulders, wrists, knees, and hips. Dinosaurs had joints like these, too.

When you plan a drawing of a moving dinosaur, try putting a series of dots where you think the joints would have been. You can then copy the drawing but move the position of the legs from the point where you put the circle marking the joint.

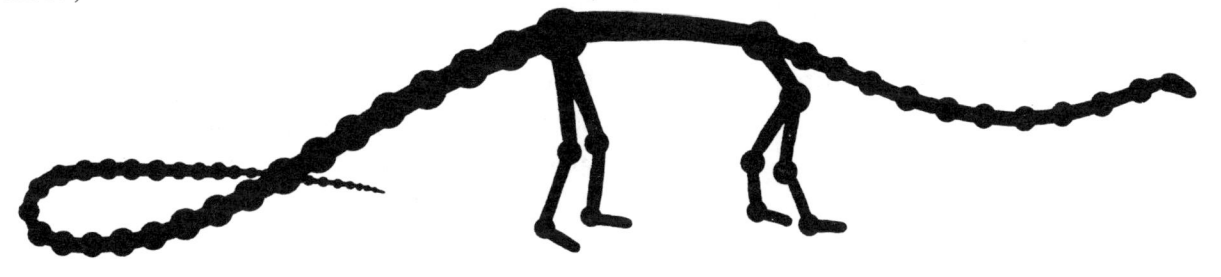

The **Diplodocus** (dip-low-doh-kus) on page 74 had lots of joints in its neck to help it reach up and turn round.

Take some scrap paper and draw the shapes of some of the dinosaurs in this book as stick figures only. Then do other stick drawings to show how the legs would be positioned when these creatures ran, jumped or reached up.

©DIAGRAM

With X-ray eyes

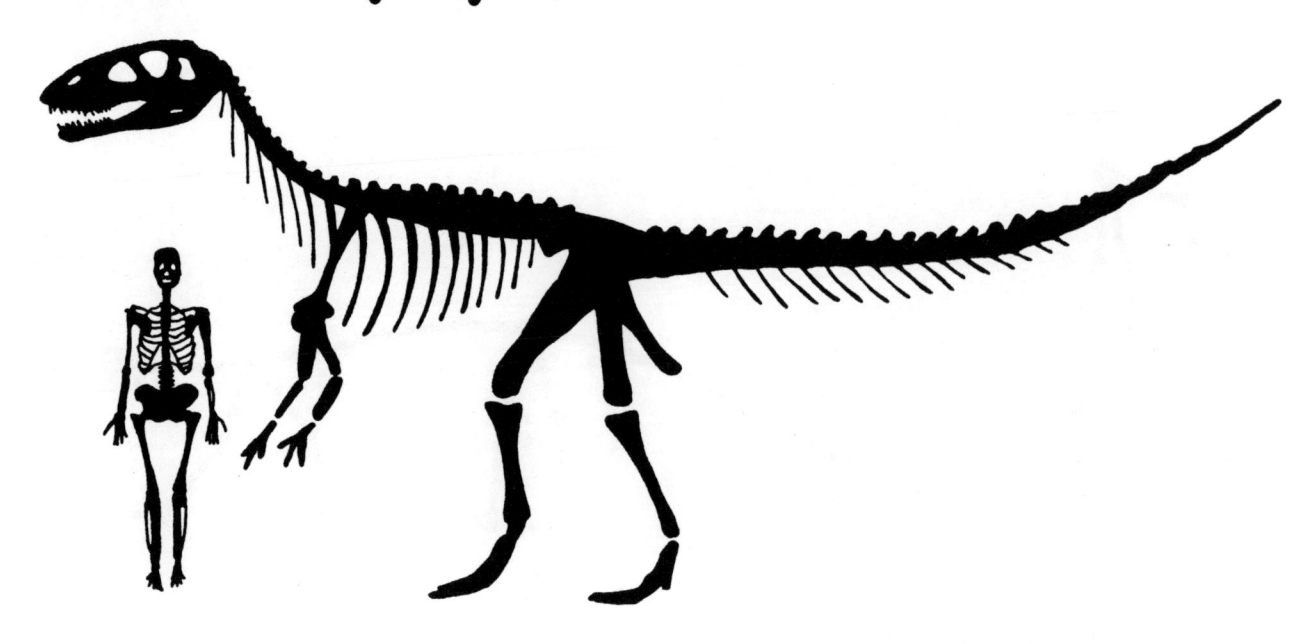

On this page, Darren has drawn the skeleton of a **Megalosaurus** (meg-a-low-saw-rus) standing beside the skeleton of a man. Below, he has also drawn the outline of a man and an outline of the same dinosaur so that you can see what its body shape was like with its flesh on.

No scientist has ever seen a live dinosaur. So they have had to guess what they looked like by putting together the bones they have found and making them into whole dinosaur skeletons.

Copy or trace the outline, and then add some skin texture. You can find another artist's idea of what this dinosaur probably looked like on page 123.

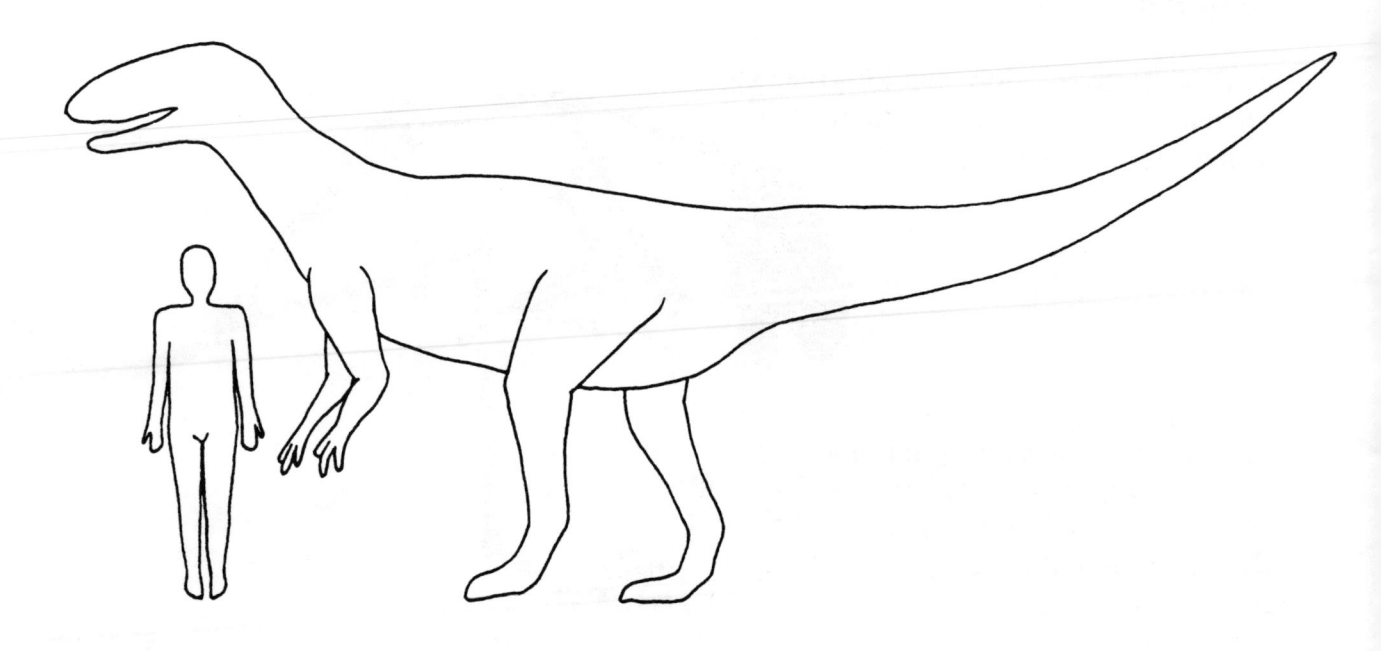

Can you imagine what this creature must have looked like in its skin? It is the skeleton of a **Triceratops** (try-ser-a-tops) which you can see on page 15. Place your tracing paper over the skeleton, and draw round the bones. Then draw round the traced skeleton to give the outline of this hideous monster.

This **Ouranosaurus** (oo-ran-oh-saw-rus) had a large fin on its spine, rather like the **Dimetrodon** (di-met-roh-don) which you can see on page 133.

©DIAGRAM

Tin-can dinosaurs

Sometimes it can be helpful to think of a dinosaur as a collection of objects like balls, eggs, tubes, boxes or tin cans, just like those drawn here.

This is a drawing of a **Smilodon** (smile-oh-don) which you can also find on page 78. But here it is made up of tin cans.

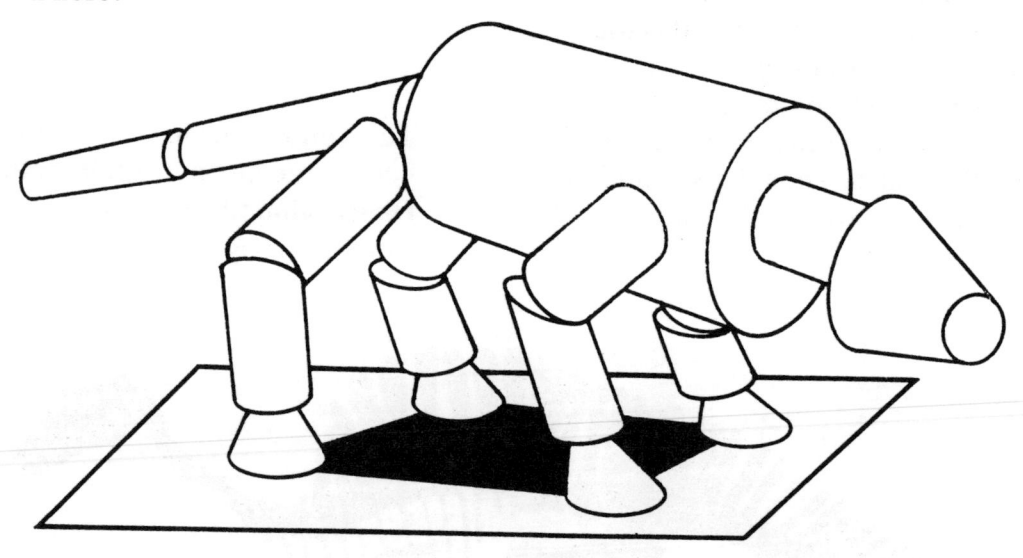

When you plan a tin can drawing, remember that legs on either side of the body are really the same size. But if one leg is nearest to you, you will need to draw that one a bit bigger. This is true whether you are drawing people, a chair, a table . . . or a dinosaur.

On the facing page there are four different prehistoric creatures that have been drawn with tin-can bodies. Flip through the book and see if you can tell which they are.

You might like to try drawing the **Megatherium** (meg-a-there-ee-um) on page 77 in this way.

61

Point of view

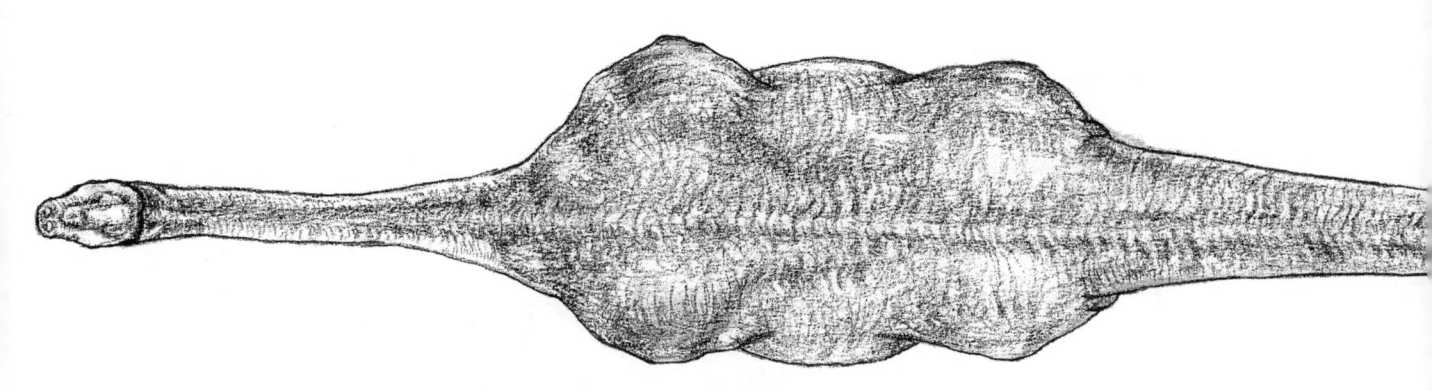

If you saw him from above

Dinosaurs often look a completely different shape depending upon your point of view. Even the simple shape of the **Diplodocus** (dip-low-doh-kus) looks completely different if you imagine you are standing behind him, in front of him, or alongside him. (You can see a side view of him on page 74.)

If you saw him from the side

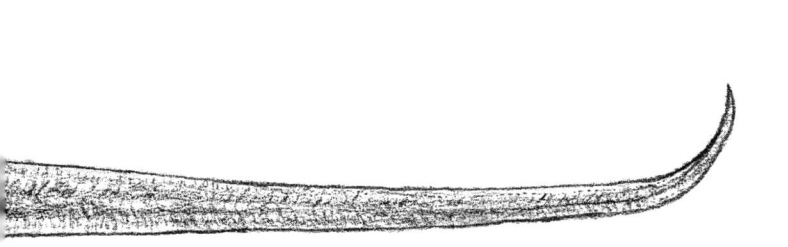

Trace or copy the outlines of the **Dromiceiomimus** (drom-mick-eye-oh-meem-us) on page 87 and the **Stenonychosaurus** (sten-on-itch-oh-saw-rus) on page 131. Then try to draw what you think they might have looked like from the front, from behind and from above.

Try to draw, too, what you think the **Struthiosaurus** (stru-thee-oh-saw-rus) on page 105 would have looked like if he was coming straight towards you.

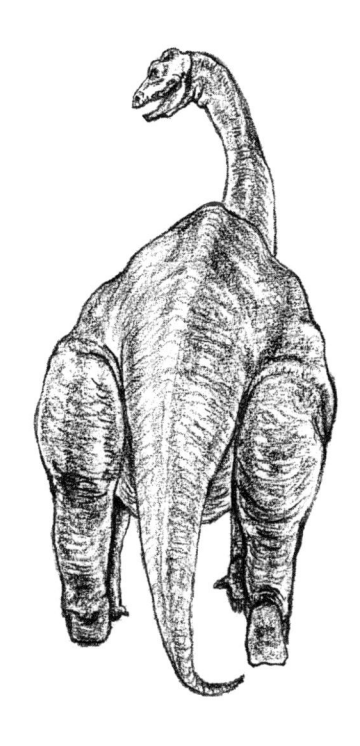

If you stood behind him

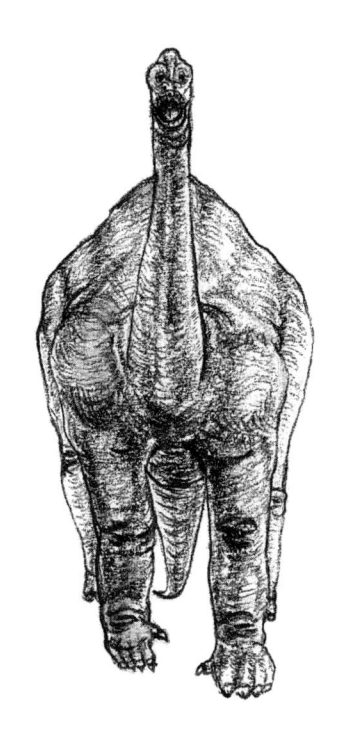

If you stood in front of him

©DIAGRAM

Part 4

Now it's time to start drawing some of the many types of dinosaurs that once roamed the Earth. It is fun and easy to do in step-by-step stages.

When you have drawn your dinosaur, there are still other things you can do with the picture. You can add skin texture in bright red, blue or green, like Mary has done to the **Stegosaurus** (steg-oh-saw-rus) from page 129.

You can also cut out a drawing made on cardboard, folding back a piece at the bottom so that it will stand up, just like Sarah has done with the **Parasaurolophus** (para-saw-roll-loaf-us). (You can find out how to draw it on pages 120–121.)

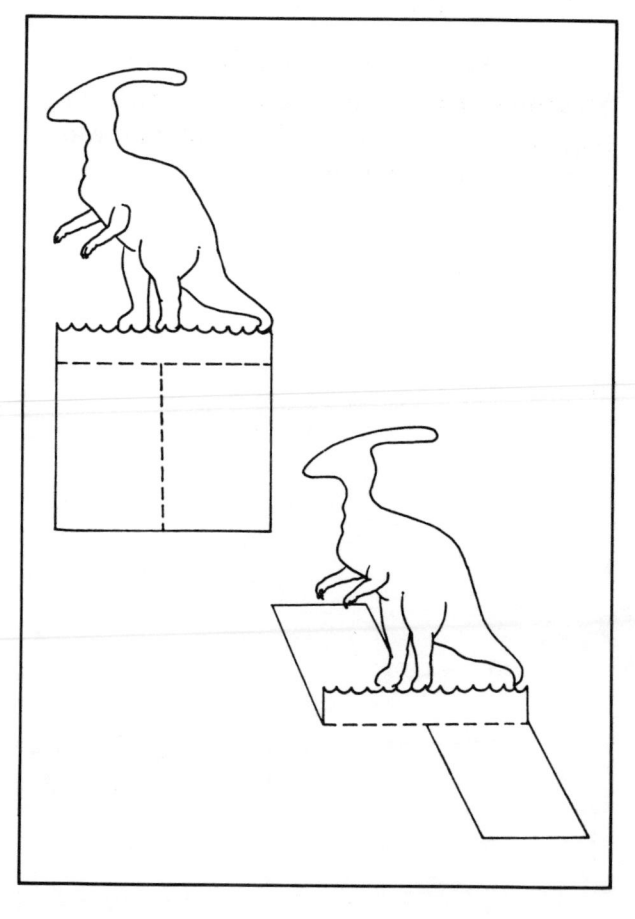

YOUR DINOSAUR GALLERY

65

You can also group dinosaurs together and show them fighting or grazing in groups. Here, for example, is a mother **Plateosaurus** (plat-ee-oh-saw-rus) with her young ones.

You can also add forest, jungle, sea or desert as a background to your drawing. The drawing below, shows a **Plesiosaur** (ples-ee-oh-saw) – which you will find on page 95 – together with three **Pteranodons** (ter-an-oh-dons) swooping down from the sky. You can see a large drawing of these huge bat-like monsters on page 119.

©DIAGRAM

A parade of prehistoric creatures

Shown here are some of the creatures that you will soon be drawing. All of them have been sketched from the side. Notice how different they all are. But we have not tried to show how large some of them were here.

You might like to copy some of these simple shapes. Later, we shall be looking at a lot of different dinosaurs in detail.

In the first row, you will find five creatures that walked on all four legs, like a dog or a cat.

Five creatures that walked on four legs

Three creatures that walked on two legs; the last creature in this row flew

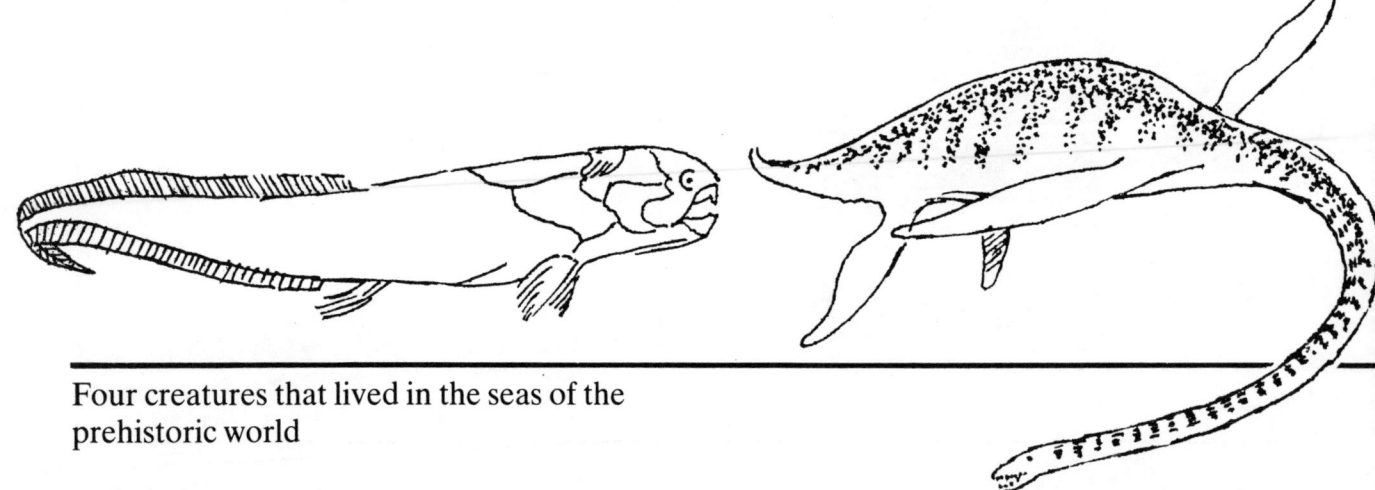

Four creatures that lived in the seas of the prehistoric world

In the next row, you can see three monsters that walked on just two legs, like a chicken. The last creature in this row flew and looked a bit like a dragonfly.

In the last row there are four creatures that lived in the seas of the prehistoric world.

©DIAGRAM

The parade continues

Look across these two pages. The first three creatures in this row are land monsters. Flip through the book and see if you can find out their names. Then see if you can identify the two creatures which are strange birds.

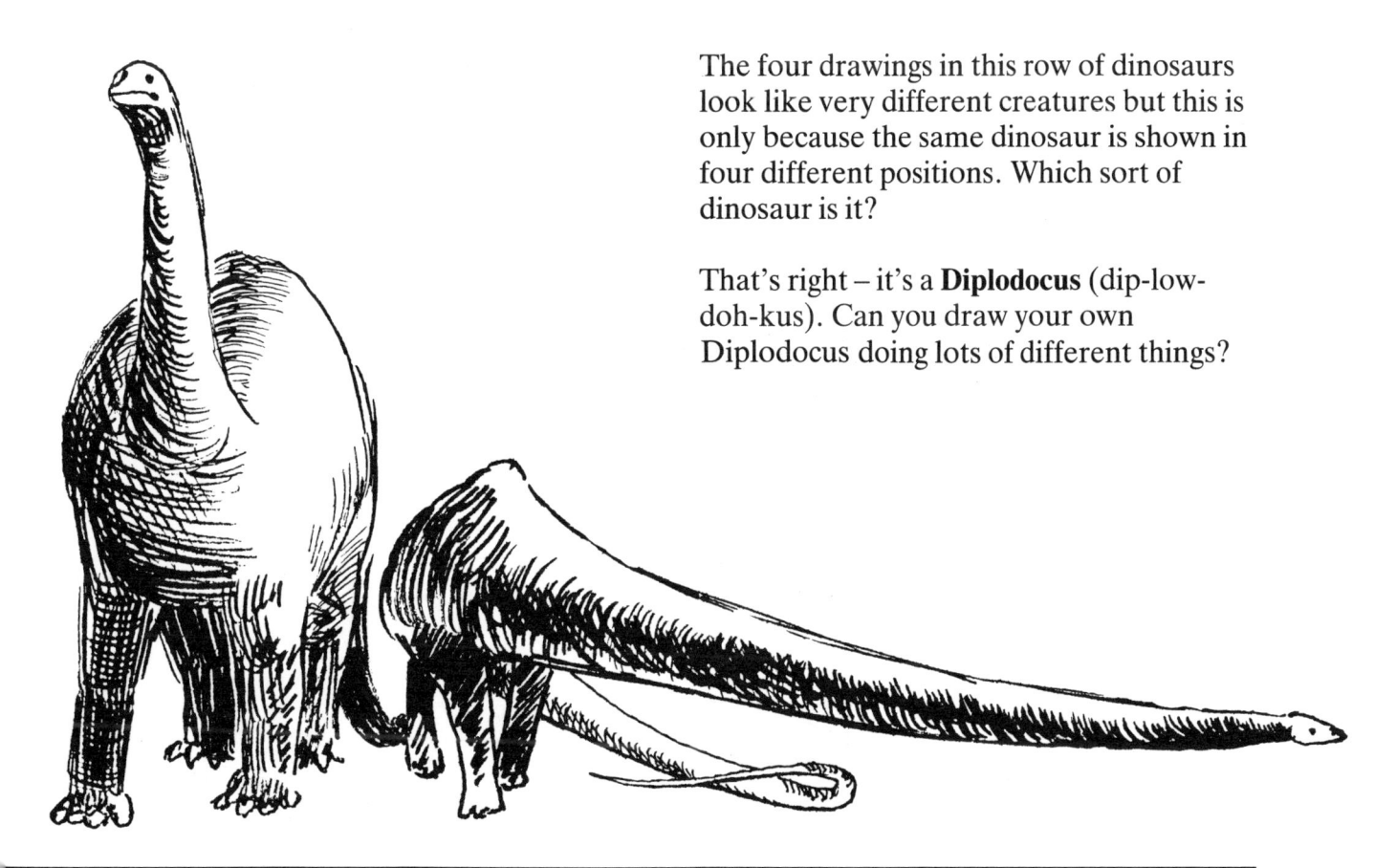

The four drawings in this row of dinosaurs look like very different creatures but this is only because the same dinosaur is shown in four different positions. Which sort of dinosaur is it?

That's right – it's a **Diplodocus** (dip-low-doh-kus). Can you draw your own Diplodocus doing lots of different things?

The final parade

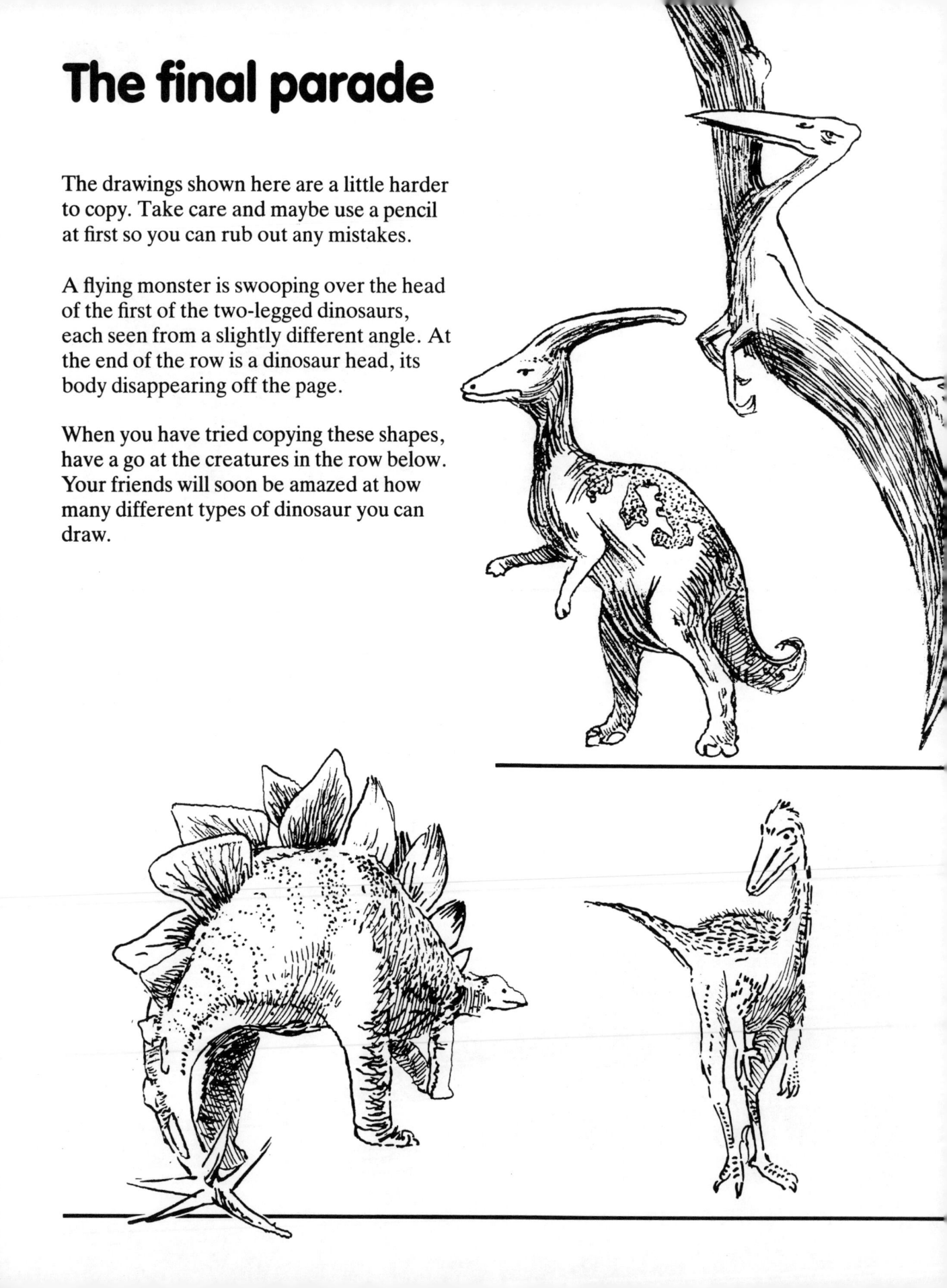

The drawings shown here are a little harder to copy. Take care and maybe use a pencil at first so you can rub out any mistakes.

A flying monster is swooping over the head of the first of the two-legged dinosaurs, each seen from a slightly different angle. At the end of the row is a dinosaur head, its body disappearing off the page.

When you have tried copying these shapes, have a go at the creatures in the row below. Your friends will soon be amazed at how many different types of dinosaur you can draw.

Now see if you can identify all the creatures on this page by flipping through the book. Can you pronounce all their names? (Remember, there are clues.)

Step-by-step

Building up your drawings of dinosaurs step-by-step makes producing brilliant drawings much easier.

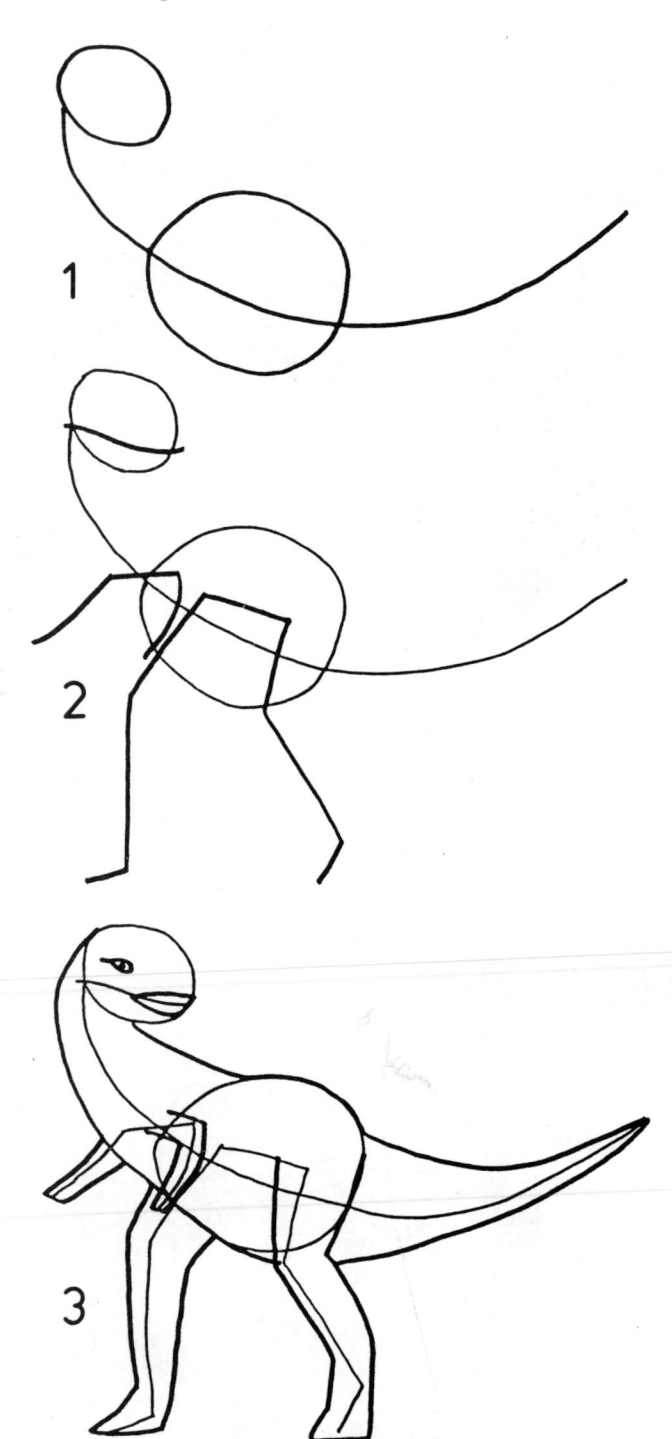

Before you start, decide on the type of dinosaur you would like to draw. Then make up your mind about whether you will be using pencils, crayons, paint, chalks or ink. This may depend on the sort of paper you have. Thin paper, remember, may not take paint very well.

It will also be best to use a soft pencil for planning your drawing.

The pages that follow show you how to construct your dinosaur drawings. Of course, you can make them any size. But all the parts of the dinosaurs' bodies must be in proportion. This means that if the tail of a dinosaur is the same length as its back leg, it must still be the same size as the back leg in a bigger drawing, too.

The three sketches on the left show how you will be learning to make dinosaur shapes from simple lines, only adding texture and detail later.

Prop up the book while you are drawing so that you do not need to keep opening it while you are copying and will not lose your page.

If you come to a part you find difficult, take your time. Draw slowly, and take care over detail.

This is a pencil drawing of a **Dilophosaurus** (dil-off-oh-saw-rus), drawn by Amanda. You can see how it was built up from the simple lines on the opposite page.

Diplodocus (dip-low-doh-kus)

Let's start with a creature with a very simple shape. Begin with an egg shape, then draw a line that sweeps right through it. Add a small oval for the head at one end. Then add stick legs and the tail. Now you can start to draw in the body, and shade it in.

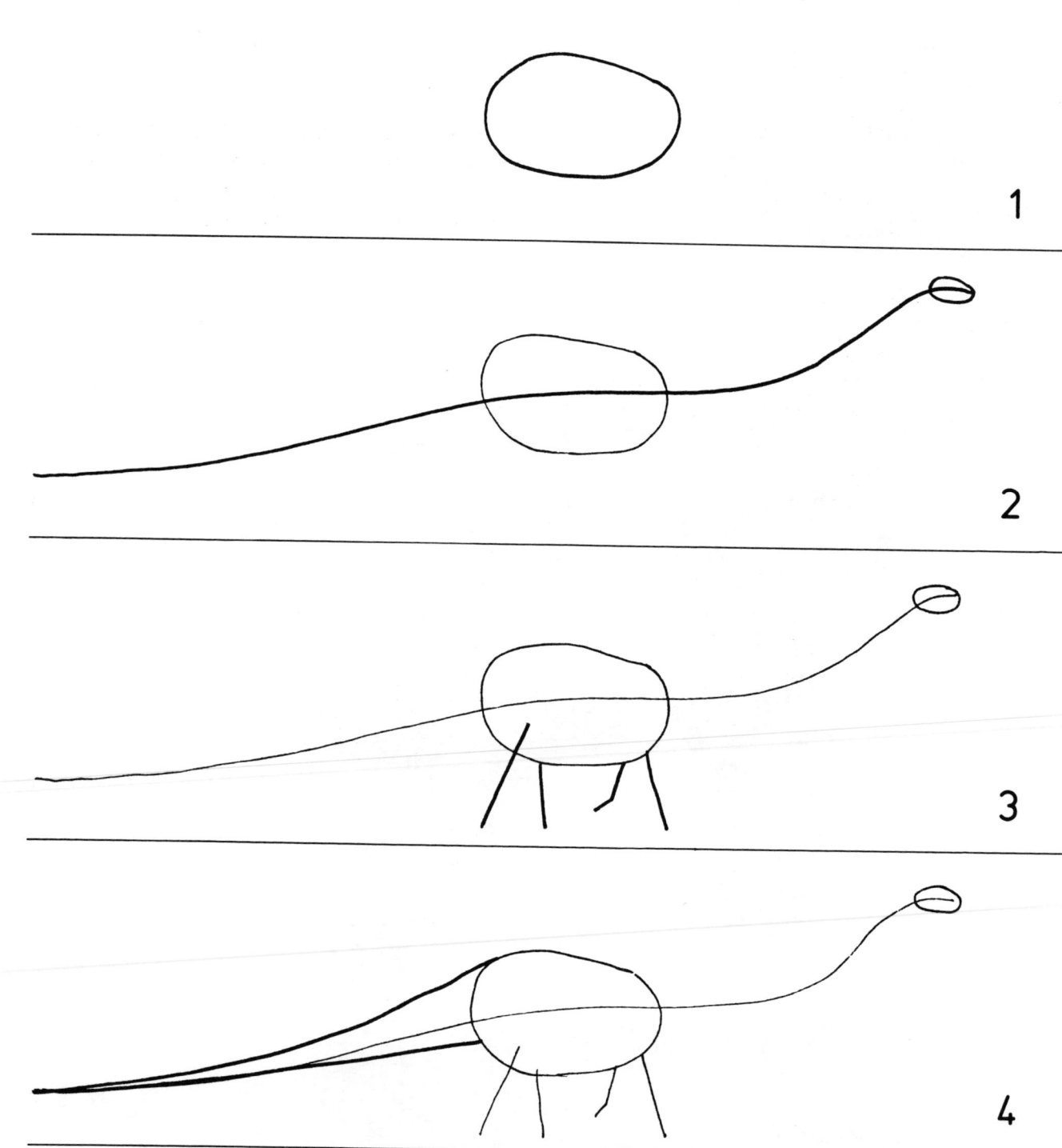

1

2

3

4

75

When you have finished your drawing, take a look at this creature's cousins on pages 111, 113, 115, and 116–117. You will then have an idea of what this beast probably looked like from the front.

5

6

7

8

©DIAGRAM

Megatherium (meg-a-there-ee-um)

This is a furry prehistoric creature that is not a dinosaur. It has a simple shape that you can build up from the outline of an egg. This drawing was made in pencil by Ryozo. I suggest that you take some scrap paper and try out all sorts of ways of making lines that look like fur before you finish the picture. Don't forget to add the long toenails.

77

Smilodon (smile-oh-don)

The **Smilodon** (smile-oh-don) had huge fangs, ate meat, and lived in Europe. This is not a dinosaur, but it was probably just as terrifying.

This creature, shown at the top of the page, was an enemy of the **Megatherium** (meg-a-there-ee-um), shown underneath it and on the previous page.

79

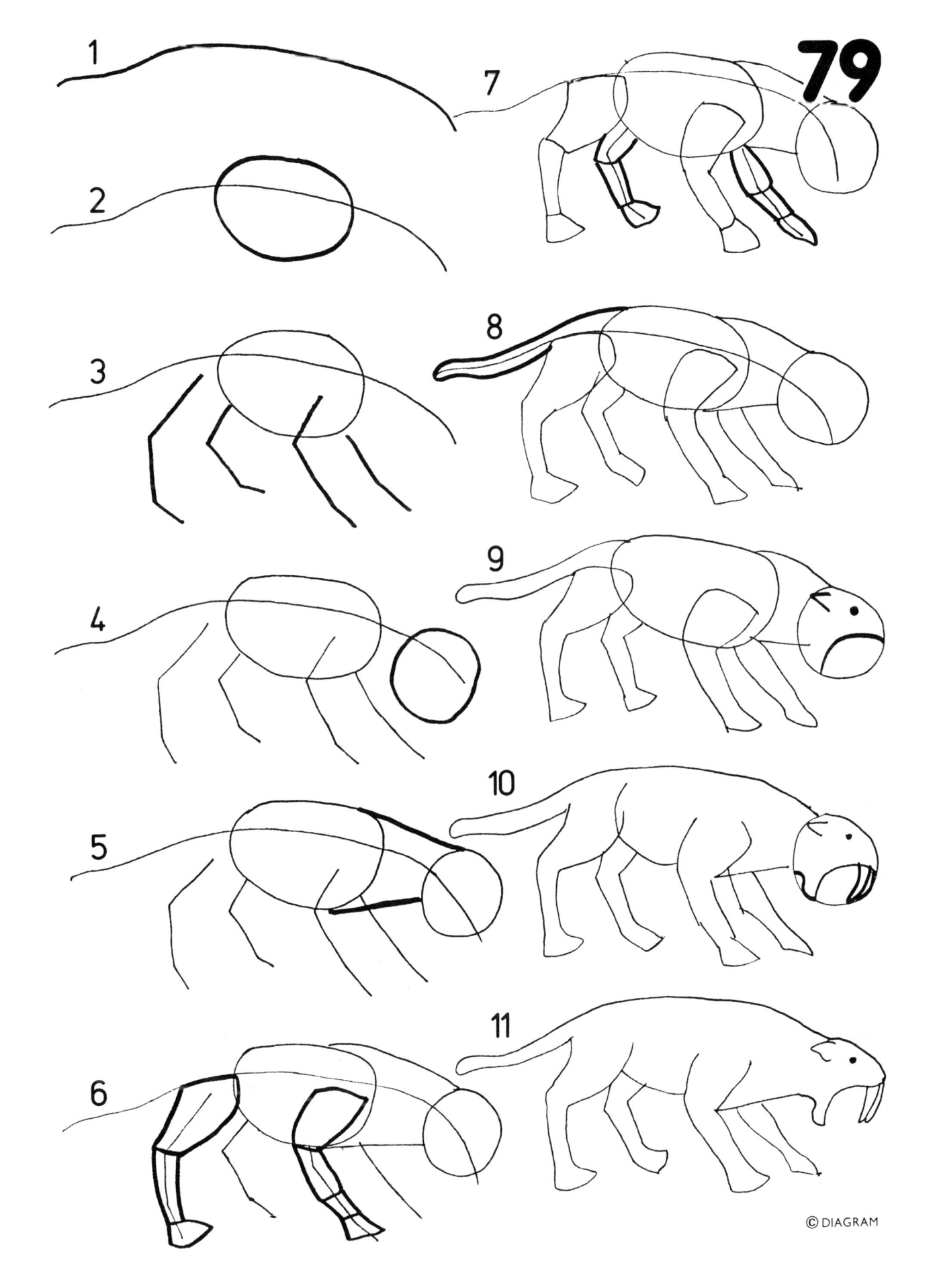

Mammuthus primigenius (mam-oo-thus pree-me-jean-ee-us)

This creature, which is sometimes called a woolly mammoth, lived long after dinosaurs had become extinct. It looked a lot like an elephant, and was chased and killed by early cavemen even though it was almost twice as tall as a human being. You will get a good effect for its fur if you use a soft pencil as Ryozo did.

81

Torosaurus (tor-oh-saw-rus)

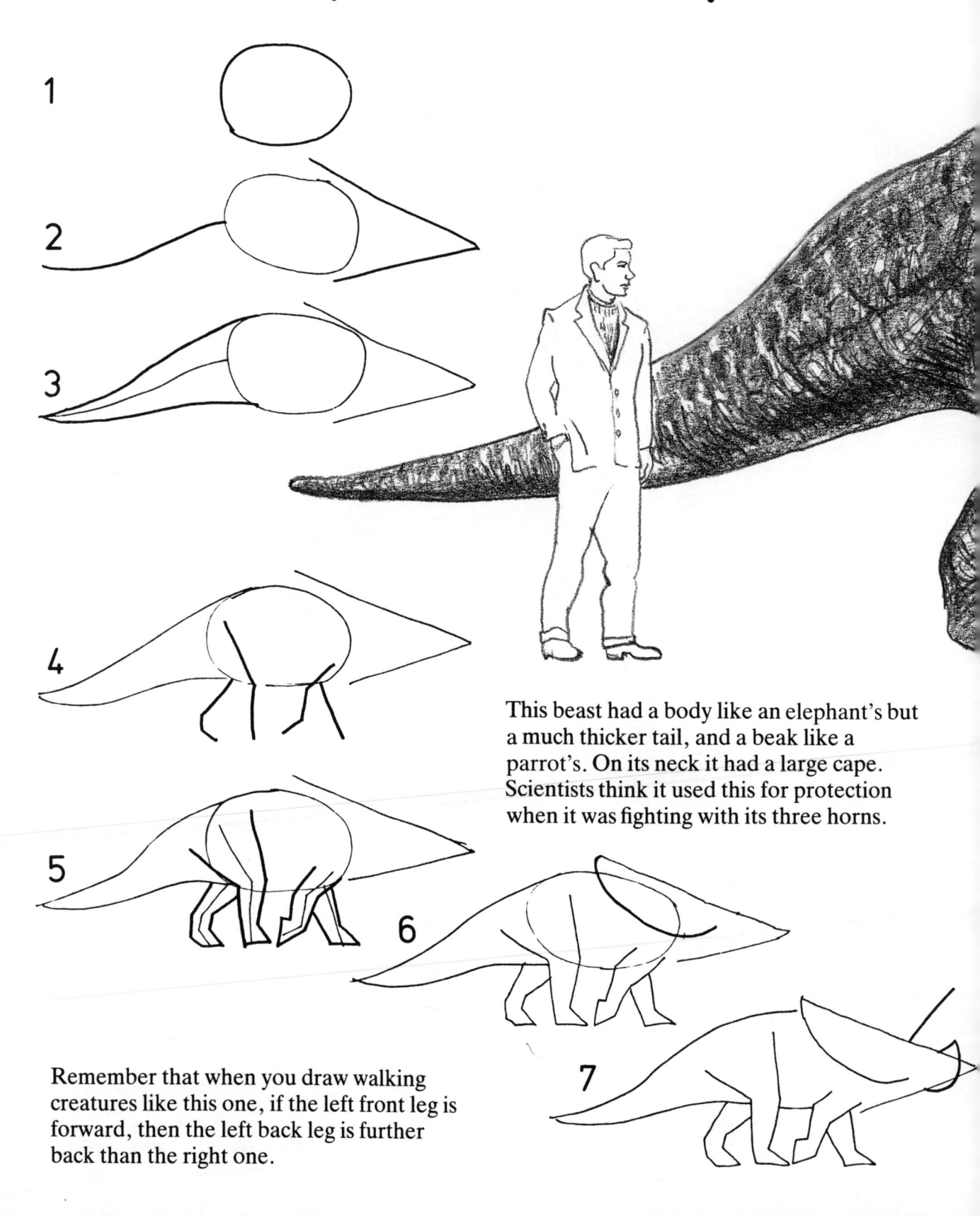

1
2
3
4
5
6
7

This beast had a body like an elephant's but a much thicker tail, and a beak like a parrot's. On its neck it had a large cape. Scientists think it used this for protection when it was fighting with its three horns.

Remember that when you draw walking creatures like this one, if the left front leg is forward, then the left back leg is further back than the right one.

83

It probably had thick, rough skin. So your drawing will need to have lots of shading to show this. Can you tell whether this drawing was made with a felt-tip, charcoal, pencil or a ballpoint?

10

9

8

This creature had an enormous head which was probably the length of a small car!

Spinosaurus (spine-oh-saw-rus)

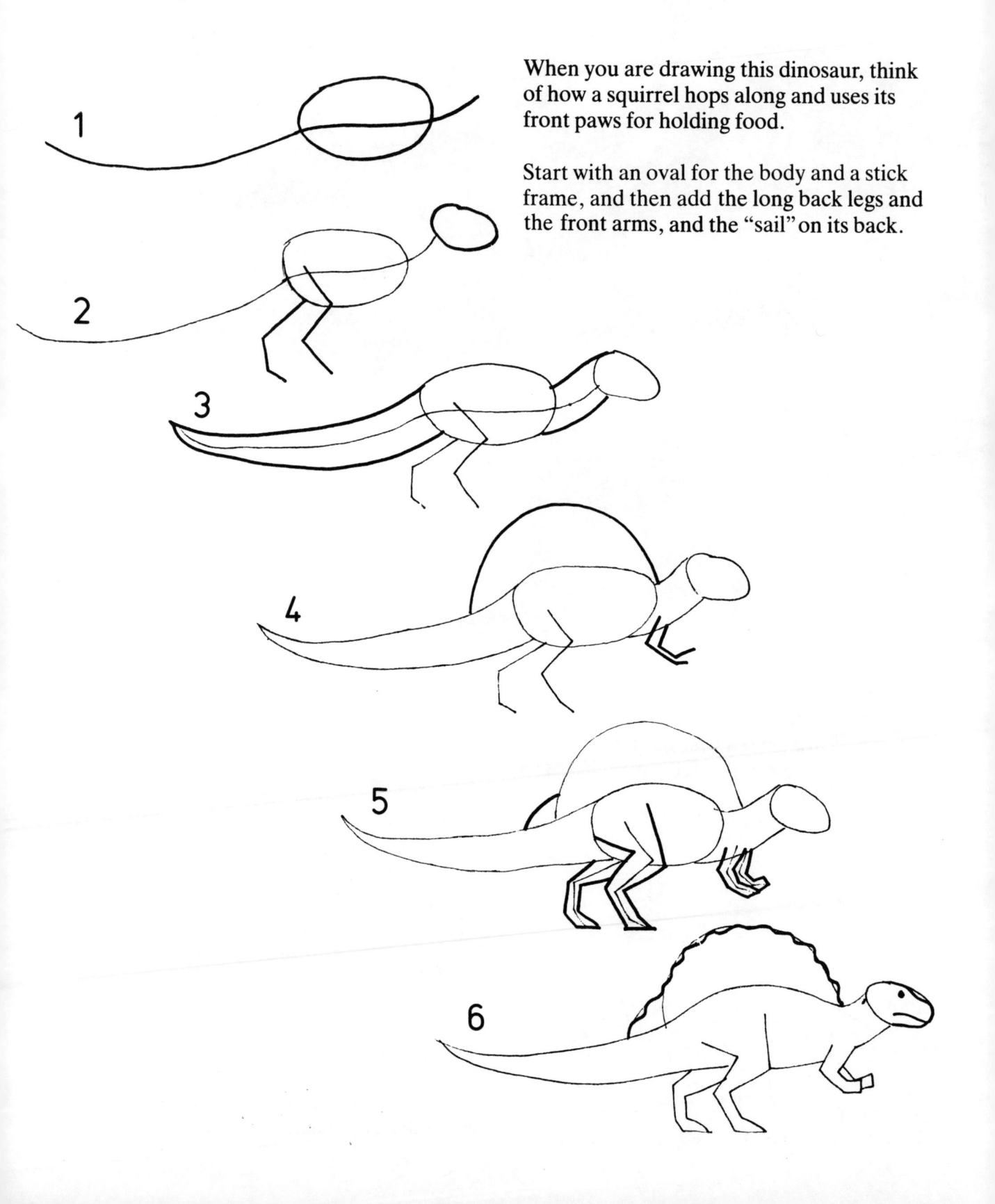

When you are drawing this dinosaur, think of how a squirrel hops along and uses its front paws for holding food.

Start with an oval for the body and a stick frame, and then add the long back legs and the front arms, and the "sail" on its back.

1

2

3

4

5

6

85

The **Spinosaurus** lived in Africa, had very sharp teeth and was gigantic in length when compared with a human being.

Perhaps try drawing this beast as it reaches up on its hind legs, or eating from the ground as shown.

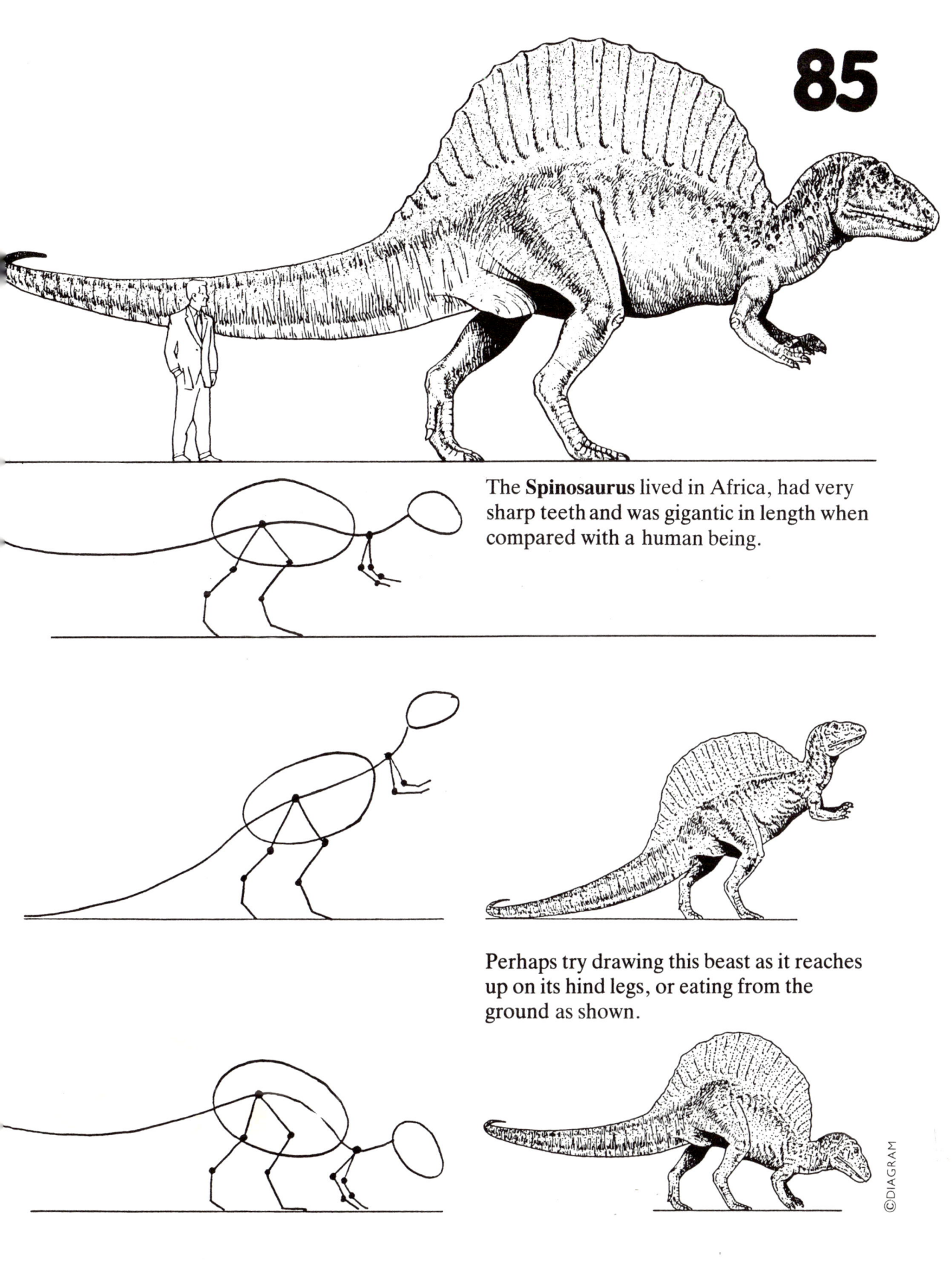

Dromiceiomimus (drom-mick-eye-oh-meem-us)

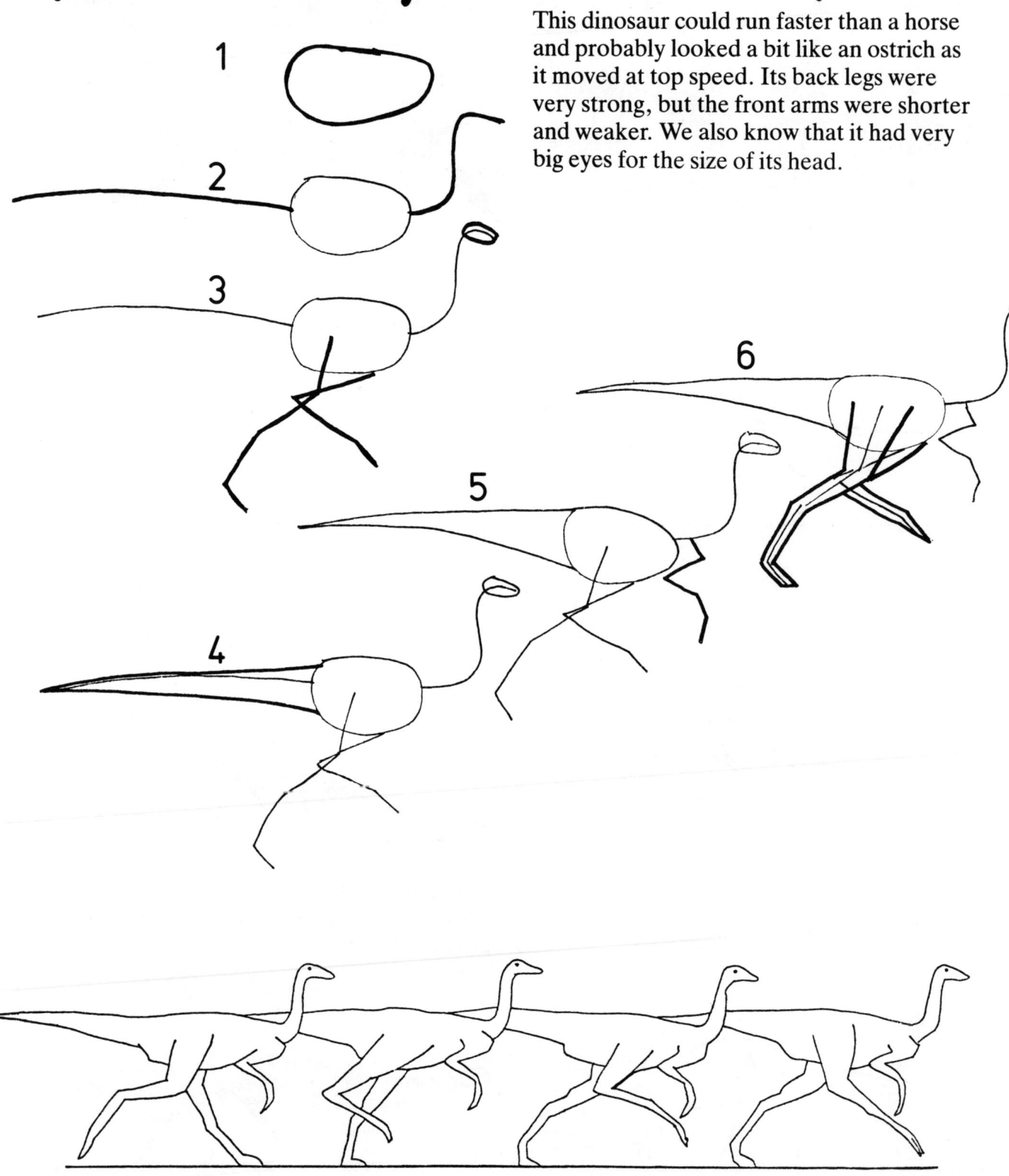

This dinosaur could run faster than a horse and probably looked a bit like an ostrich as it moved at top speed. Its back legs were very strong, but the front arms were shorter and weaker. We also know that it had very big eyes for the size of its head.

87

The **Dromiceiomimus** would certainly have won the marathon in the dinosaur Olympics!

9

8

7

Perhaps draw a whole row of these running dinosaurs going right across a page. Remember to keep one of its legs on the ground while the other is in the air.

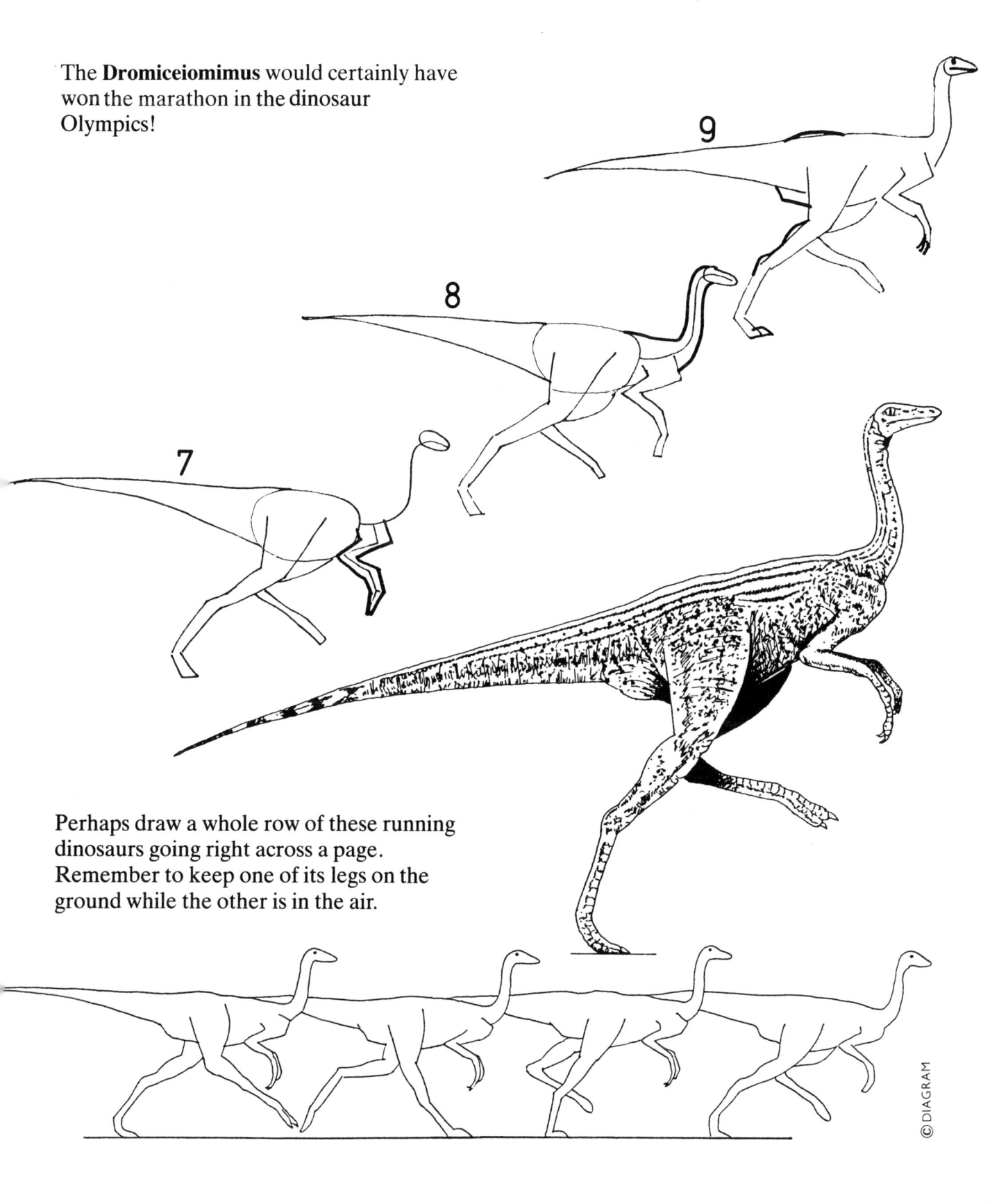

Sarcosaurus (sark-oh-saw-rus)

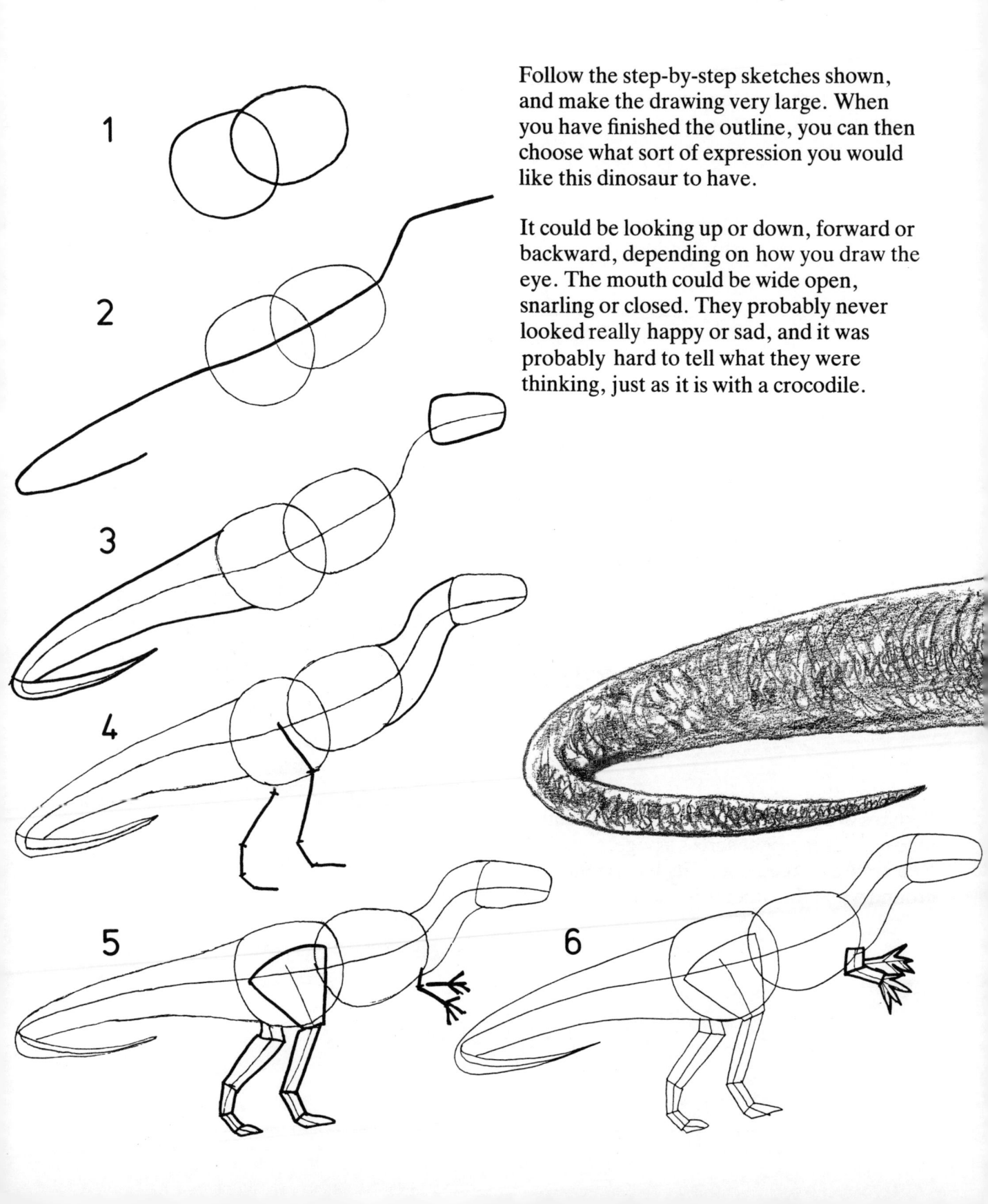

Follow the step-by-step sketches shown, and make the drawing very large. When you have finished the outline, you can then choose what sort of expression you would like this dinosaur to have.

It could be looking up or down, forward or backward, depending on how you draw the eye. The mouth could be wide open, snarling or closed. They probably never looked really happy or sad, and it was probably hard to tell what they were thinking, just as it is with a crocodile.

89

Icarosaurus (ick-a-roh-saw-rus)

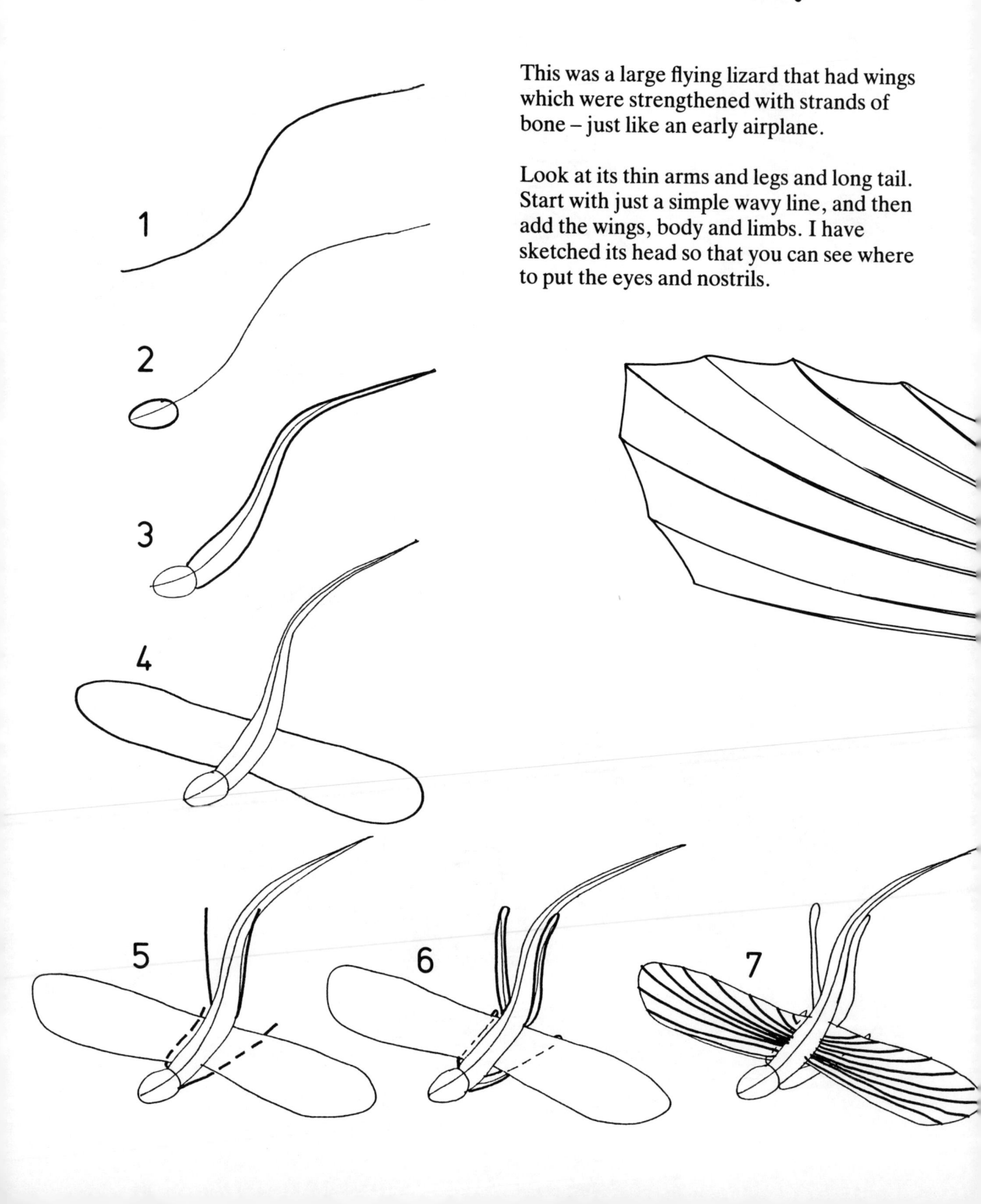

This was a large flying lizard that had wings which were strengthened with strands of bone – just like an early airplane.

Look at its thin arms and legs and long tail. Start with just a simple wavy line, and then add the wings, body and limbs. I have sketched its head so that you can see where to put the eyes and nostrils.

91

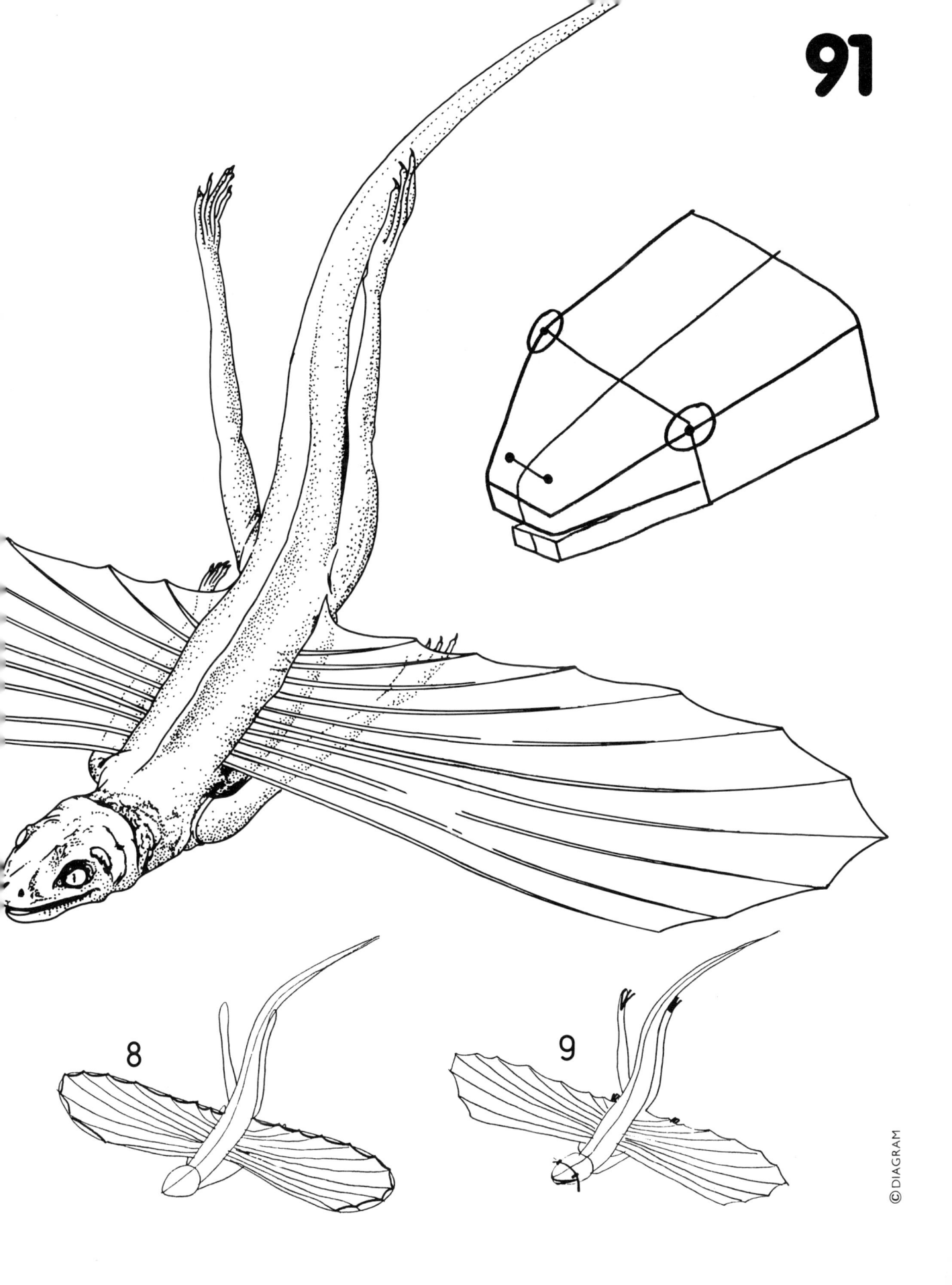

8

9

Dunkleosteus (dunk-lay-os-tay-us)

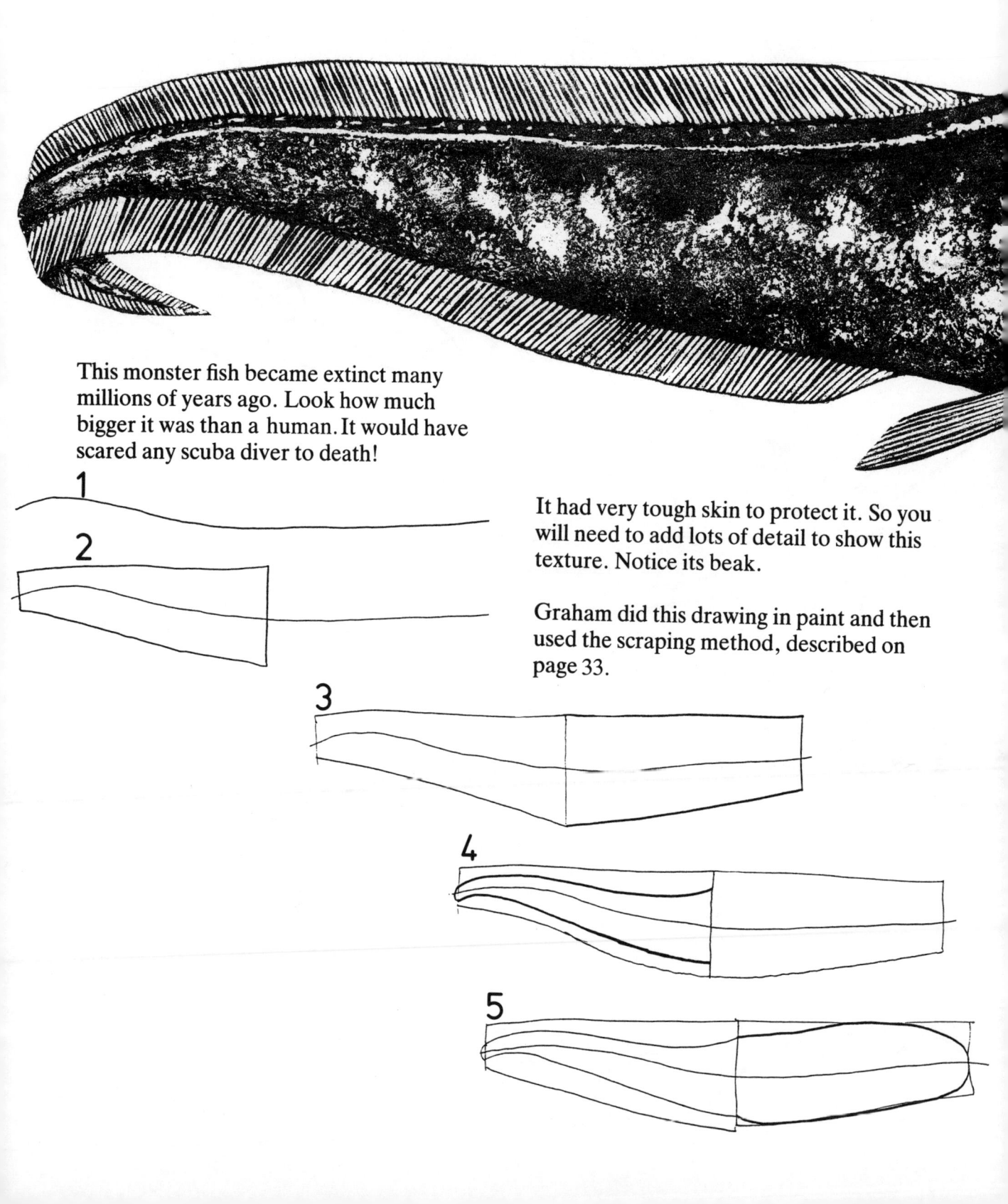

This monster fish became extinct many millions of years ago. Look how much bigger it was than a human. It would have scared any scuba diver to death!

It had very tough skin to protect it. So you will need to add lots of detail to show this texture. Notice its beak.

Graham did this drawing in paint and then used the scraping method, described on page 33.

93

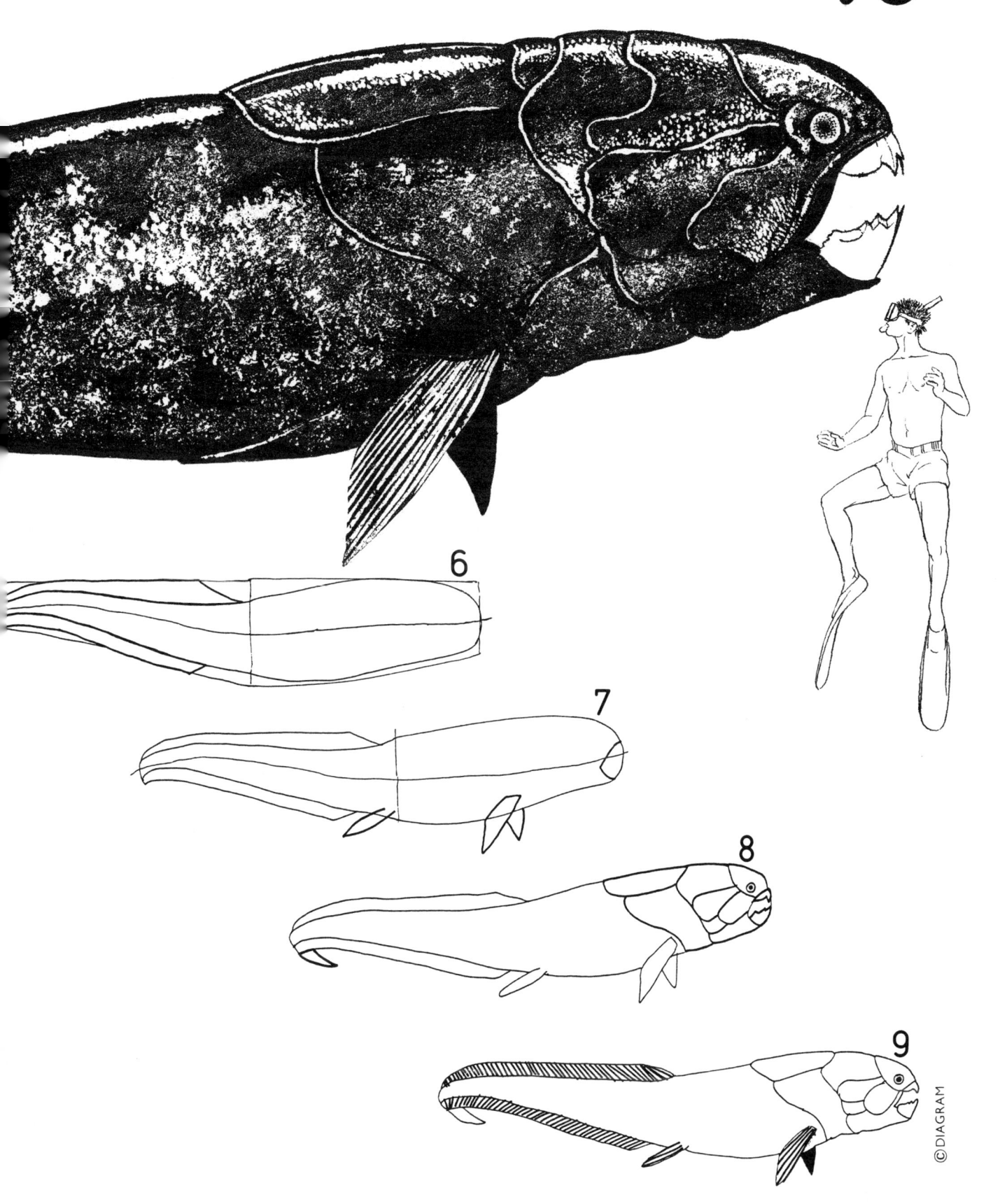

6

7

8

9

Plesiosaur (ples-ee-oh-saw)

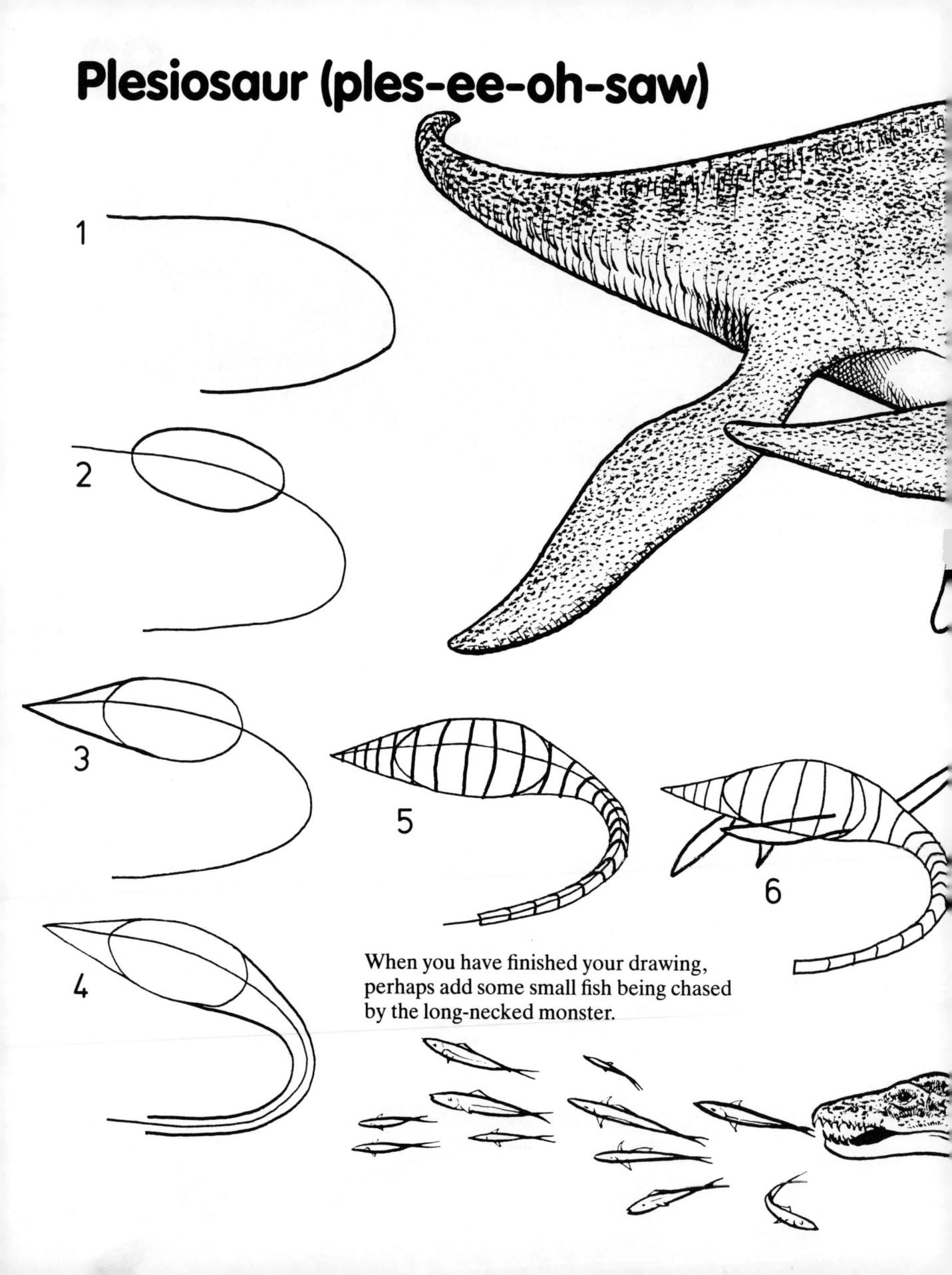

1
2
3
4
5
6

When you have finished your drawing, perhaps add some small fish being chased by the long-necked monster.

95

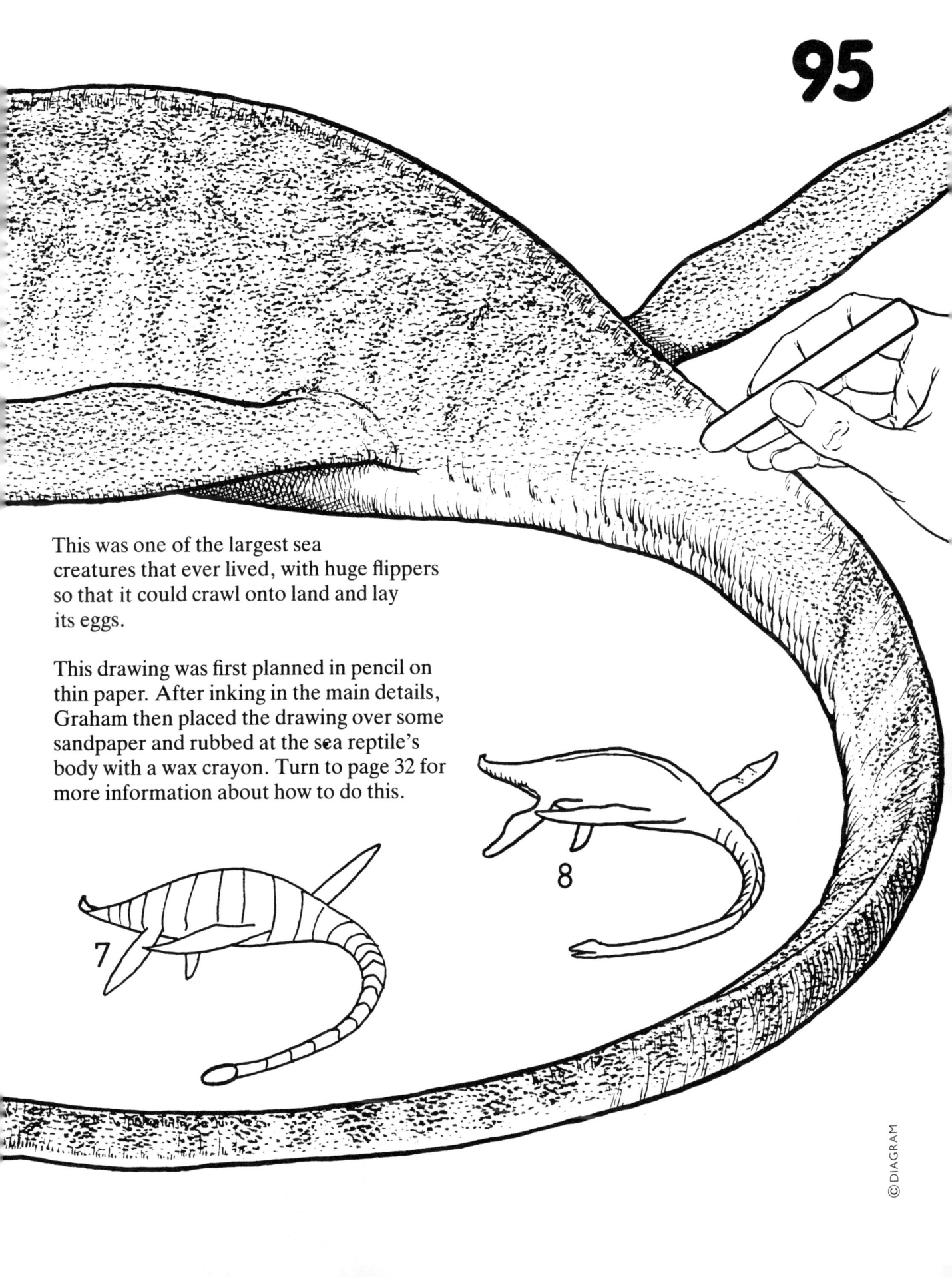

This was one of the largest sea creatures that ever lived, with huge flippers so that it could crawl onto land and lay its eggs.

This drawing was first planned in pencil on thin paper. After inking in the main details, Graham then placed the drawing over some sandpaper and rubbed at the sea reptile's body with a wax crayon. Turn to page 32 for more information about how to do this.

Tylosaurus (tile-oh-saw-rus)

This is another huge prehistoric sea monster with sharp teeth and a spiny back.
Look how much bigger he was than the diver!

1
2
3
4

97

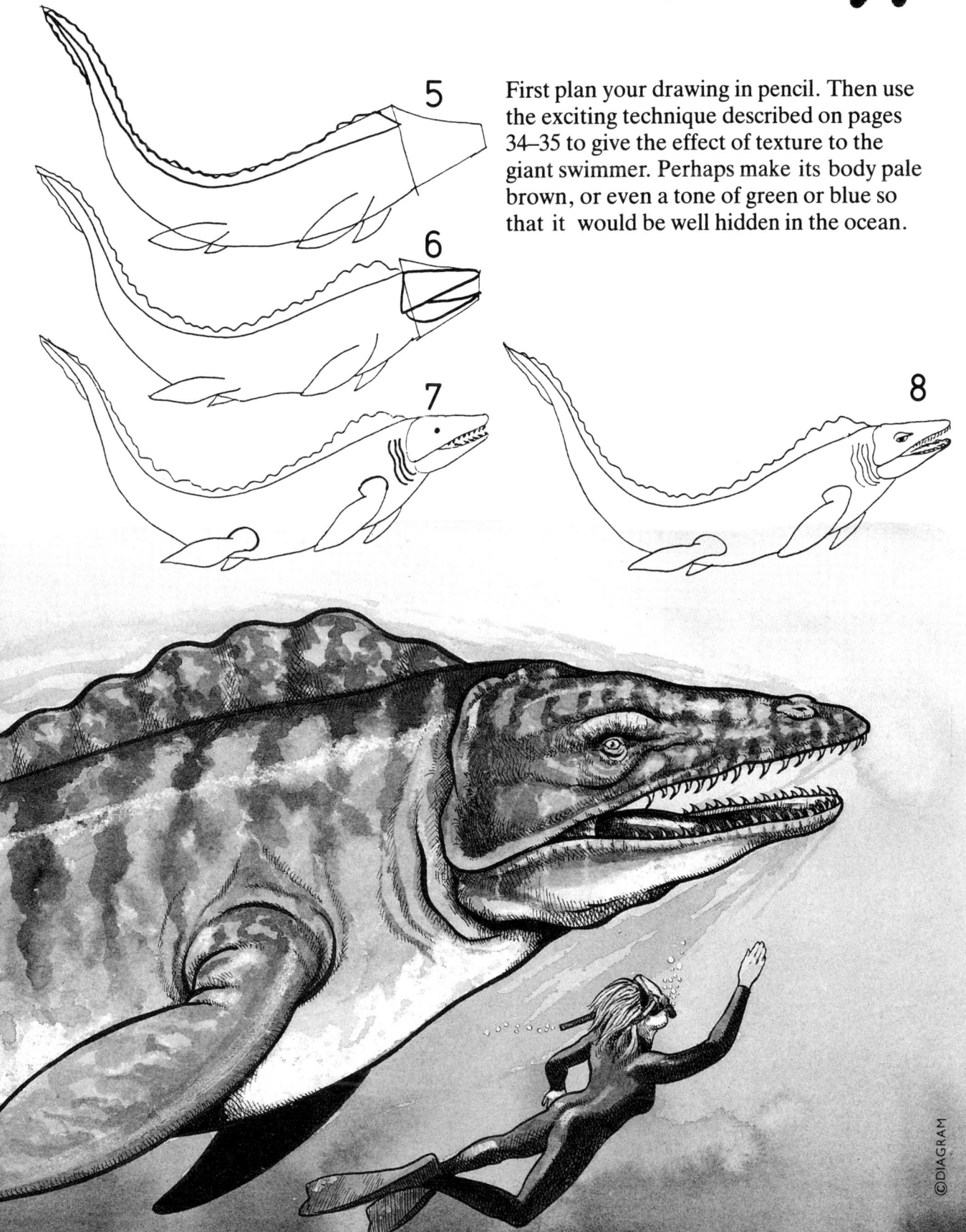

5

6

7

8

First plan your drawing in pencil. Then use the exciting technique described on pages 34–35 to give the effect of texture to the giant swimmer. Perhaps make its body pale brown, or even a tone of green or blue so that it would be well hidden in the ocean.

Placodus (plak-oh-dus)

This prehistoric creature was a bit like a lizard and probably lived in shallow, swampy water. First work on the outline and then make marks all over the body with a felt-tip to give the effect of mottled skin. Look at the page opposite to see a detail of the drawing.

99

Tyrannosaurus (tie-ran-oh-saw-rus) skeleton

This must be the best known dinosaur of all – big, very fierce and like a creature from a horror film. The skeleton here looks hard to draw. But it is really very easy if you build up the frame from its basic parts, adding detail later. On pages 124–125, you can see how to draw a **Tyrannosaurus** with its flesh on!

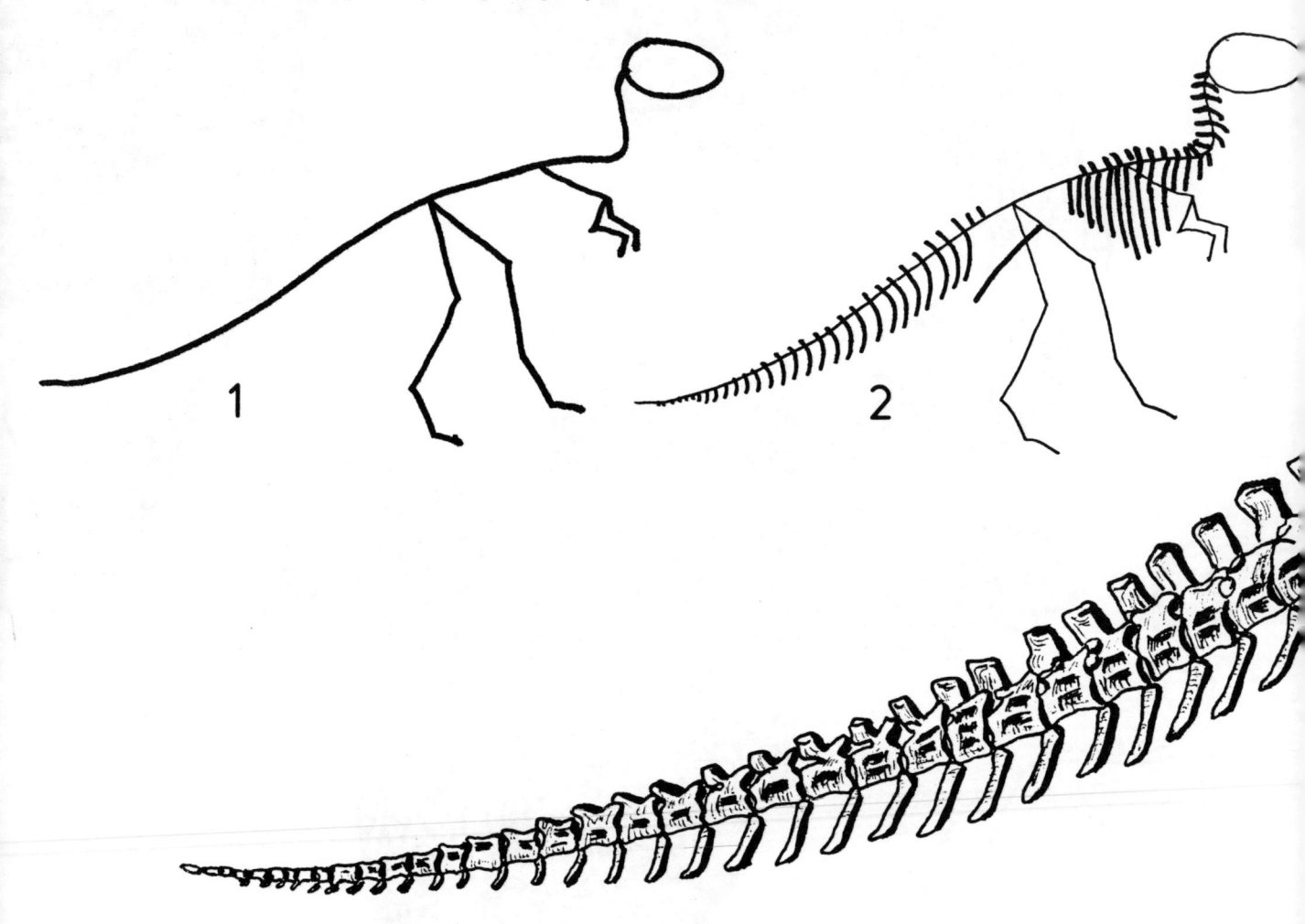

1

2

When you shade in the bones, always be sure to keep the dark areas on the same side of the skeleton. This drawing was planned with a pencil, and then built up with a felt-tip.

101

3

Stegosaurus (steg-oh-saw-rus)

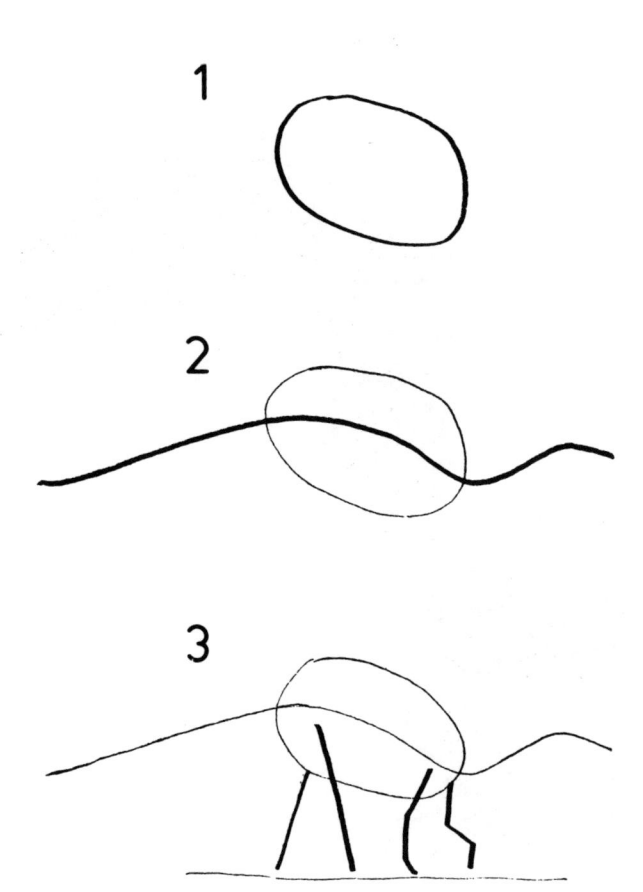

This creature had a fat, round body and legs like an elephant's, but a small head and long tail. Down its back were two rows of large flat spikes which were probably used to keep its body cool in the heat.

First plan the body shape with a simple oval. Then add the legs, tail, neck and head.

Next, on pencil lines drawn above the body, measure out a row of points to mark where the spikes should be. The larger ones should be in the middle of the back, and the smaller ones at the front and the tail end. (You can rub out these lines later.)

Now draw the spikes on the creature's back, with another row of smaller ones by their side. They would run right down the creature's back, too.

On page 129 there is a picture of a **Stegosaurus** walking away from you.

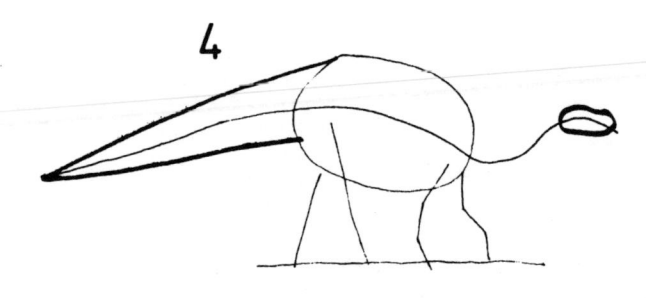

103

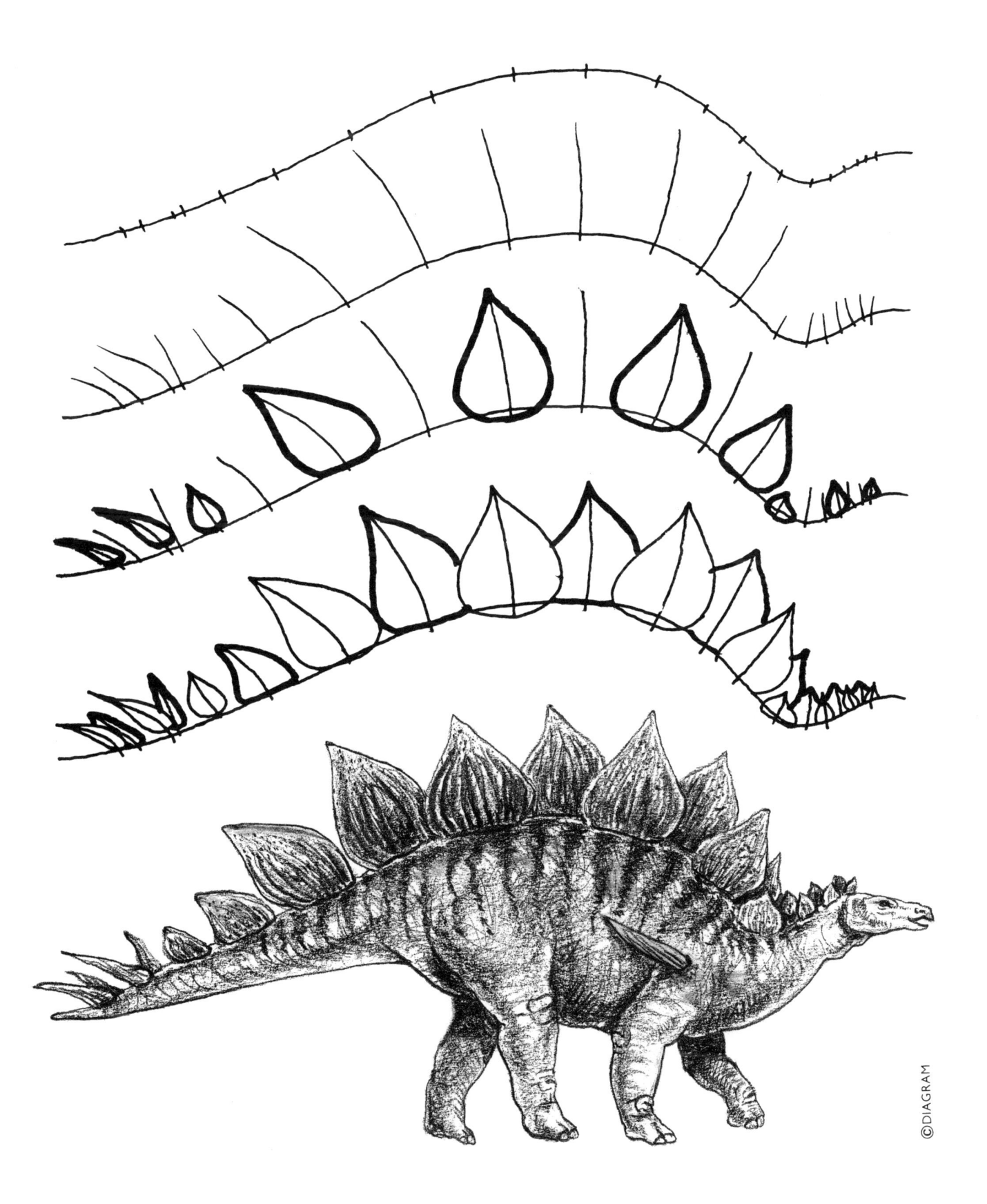

Struthiosaurus (stru-thee-oh-saw-rus)

This strange beast was a bit like a large tortoise with long legs under its body. It also had a row of spikes set all around the edges of its shell back. To draw a side view, start to build it up from a simple egg shape for the central body area.

1

2

3

4

7

8

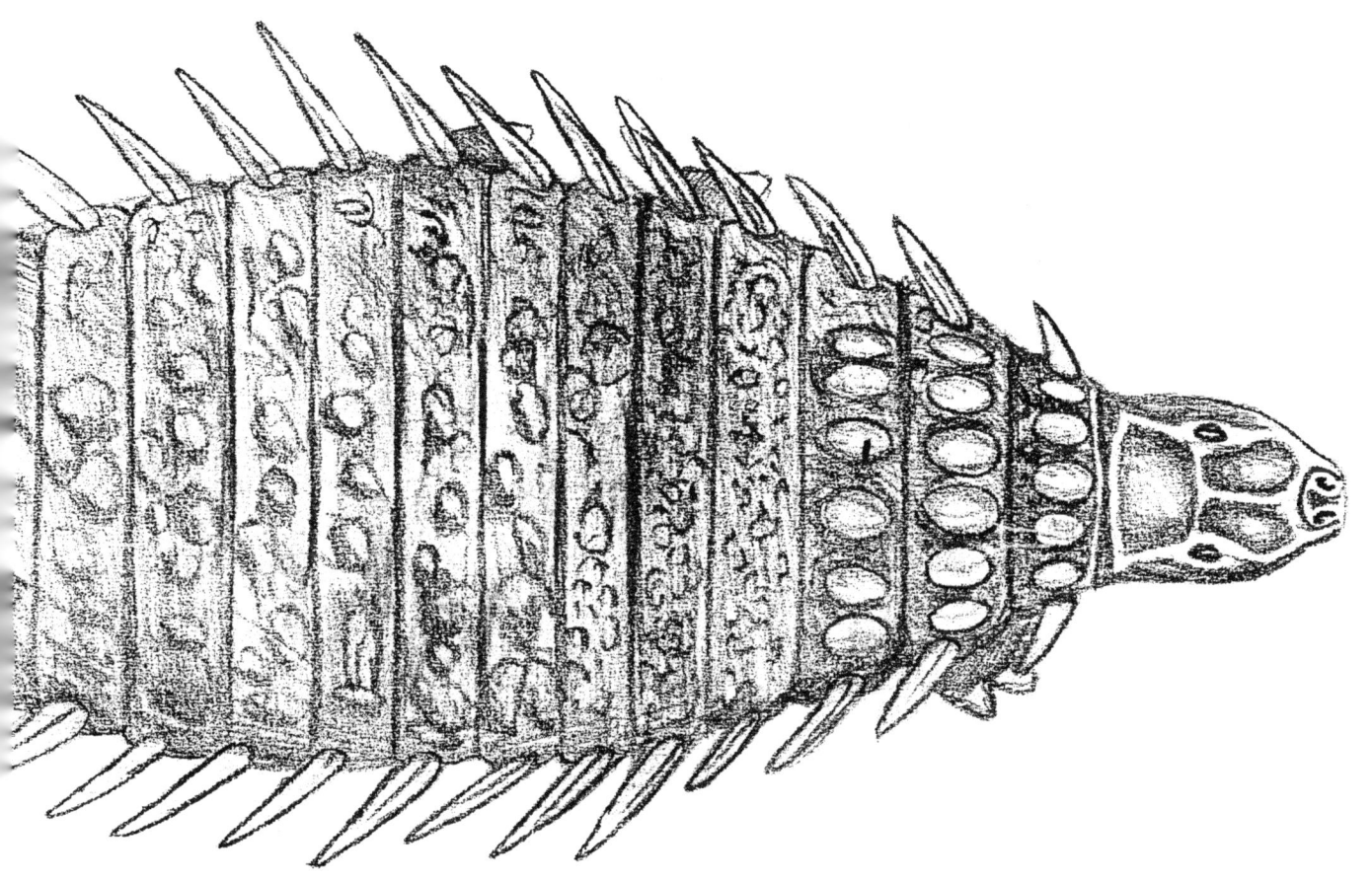

105

This is what a **Struthiosaurus** may have looked like from the top.

5

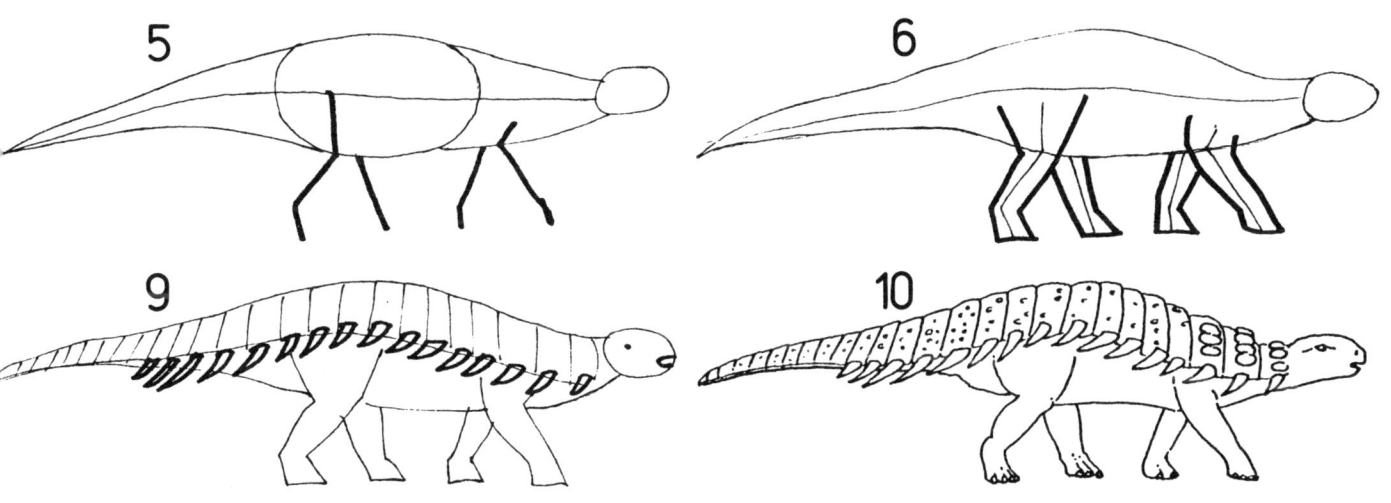

6

9

10

©DIAGRAM

Archaeopteryx (ark-ay-op-ter-ricks)

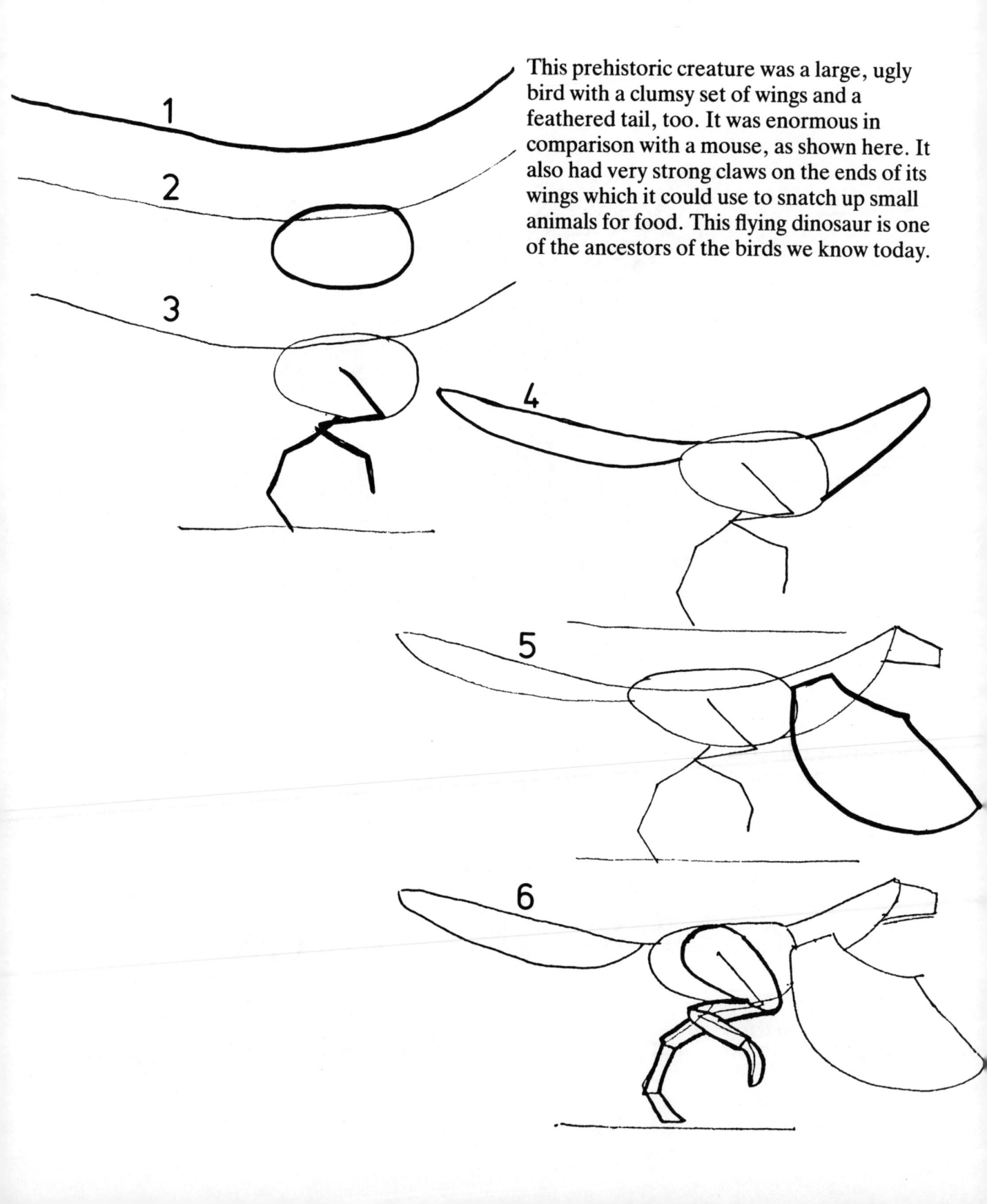

This prehistoric creature was a large, ugly bird with a clumsy set of wings and a feathered tail, too. It was enormous in comparison with a mouse, as shown here. It also had very strong claws on the ends of its wings which it could use to snatch up small animals for food. This flying dinosaur is one of the ancestors of the birds we know today.

107

There is a lot of detail for you to put in the feathers, so use a fine pen for this or work very carefully with a thin brush. This drawing was made with a fine felt-tip. Look how the legs move as it walks. It was probably not very good at flying, however.

©DIAGRAM

Phorusrhacos longissimus (for-us-ra-kus long-is-sim-us)

If you think the creature on the previous page was funny-looking, then this one is a real joke! It was a bit like a monster chicken.

After you have drawn the outline in pencil on good, strong paper, paint in the feathers using ink and a brush. Make the brush marks in the direction the feathers would grow – that means away from the body. Then give the head and legs some extra texture with dots, using the fine end of a brush.

Remember that if you press down with the brush when using the ink for the feathers, you get a thick line. But if you lift the brush off the paper, you get a thinner line.

When Graham did this drawing, he used black ink and a brush for the feathers. Then, to make it sharp, he painted carefully around some of the wing, neck and tail feathers with white paint.

Brachiosaurus
(brack-ee-oh-saw-rus)

Most of the previous dinosaurs in this part of the book were drawn from the side view and so looked a bit flat. Now we are going to start drawing lots of creatures from the side, front and back using boxes, tubes and sausage shapes to give the beasts a solid look.

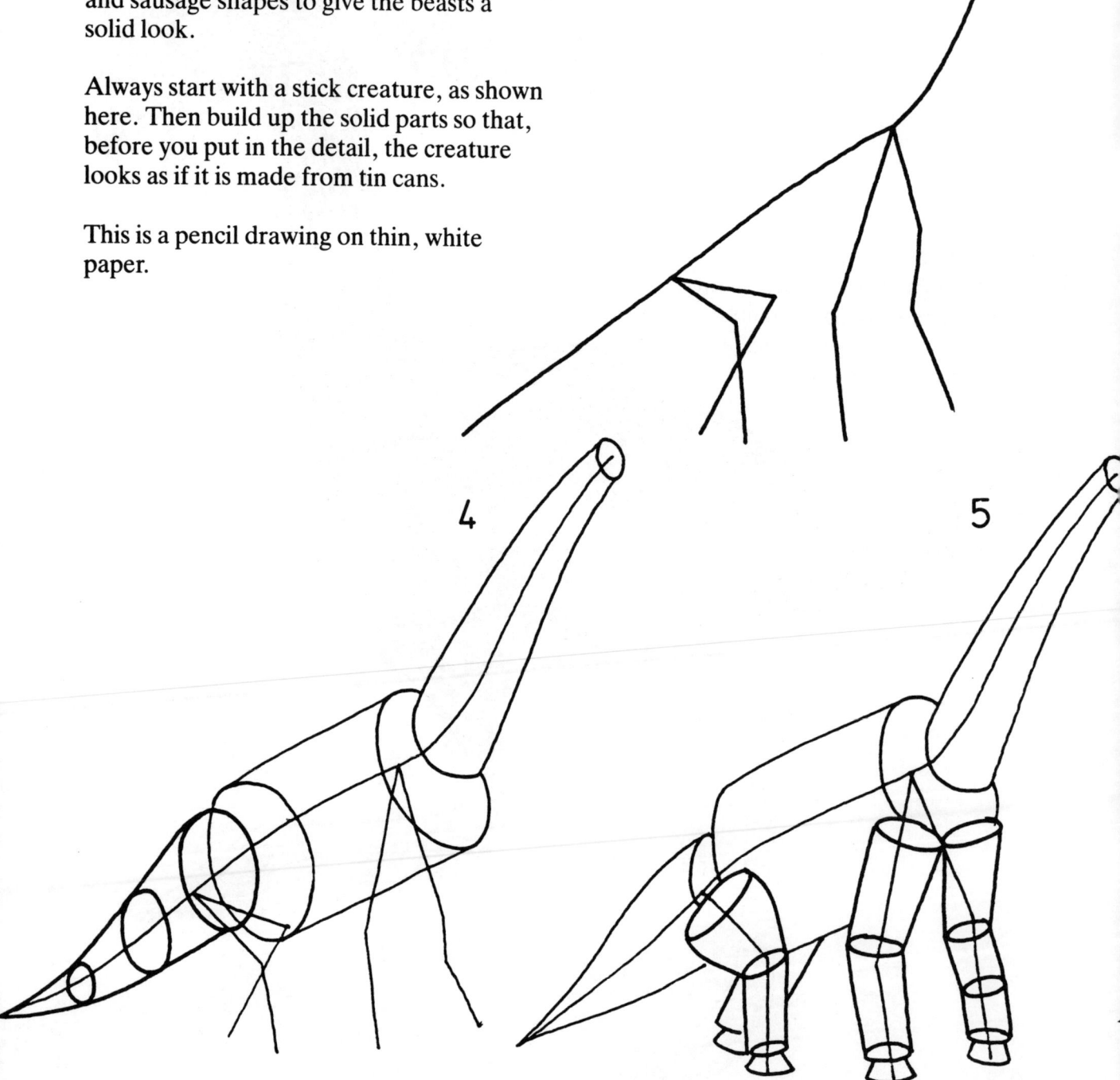

Always start with a stick creature, as shown here. Then build up the solid parts so that, before you put in the detail, the creature looks as if it is made from tin cans.

This is a pencil drawing on thin, white paper.

111

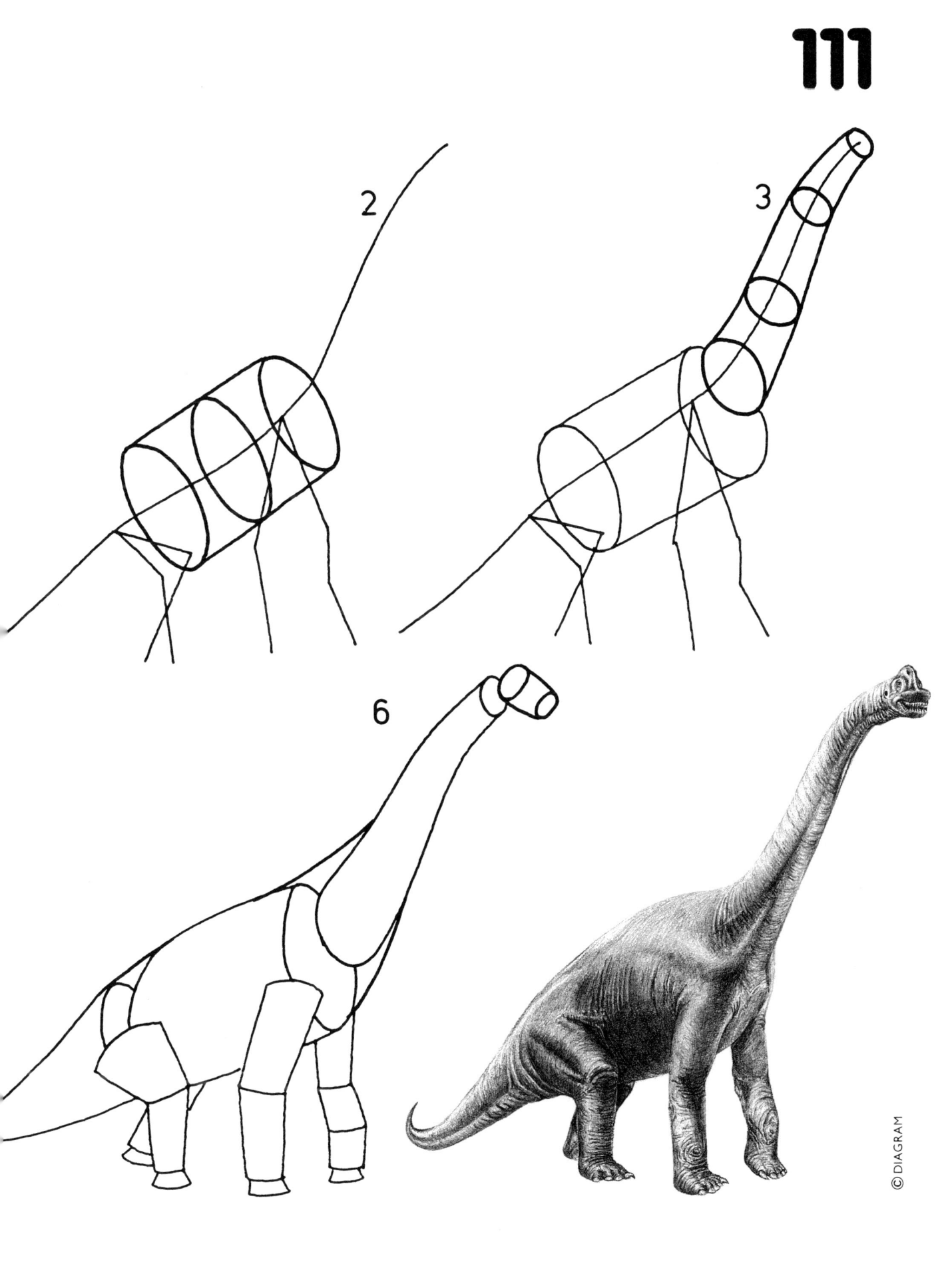

2

3

6

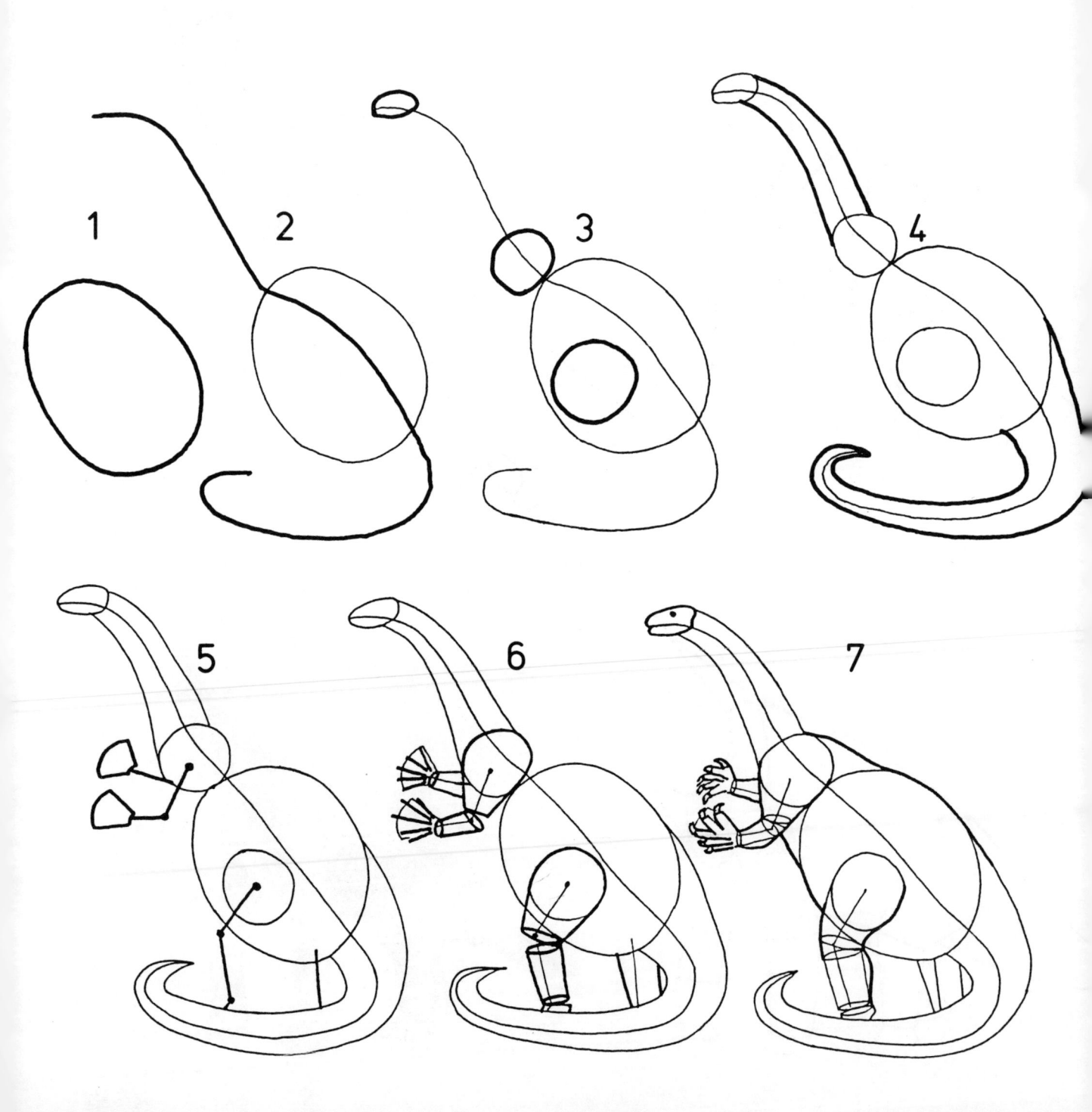

Plateosaurus (plat-ee-oh-saw-rus)

The creature drawn here is standing on its hind legs and reaching up. Notice how it used its tail as a support to help it keep its balance. (There is a front view on page 115.)

This dinosaur was longer than a bus, and its bones have been found all over Europe. It was probably a vegetarian and would rear up on its hind legs to get at leaves on trees.

It probably had skin that looked like an elephant's. So remember to draw lots of creases round the body, as if it were wrapped up in string. These wrinkle lines will also make your dinosaur look more solid. Add these details after you have finished the outline.

Plateosaurus (plat-ee-oh-saw-rus)

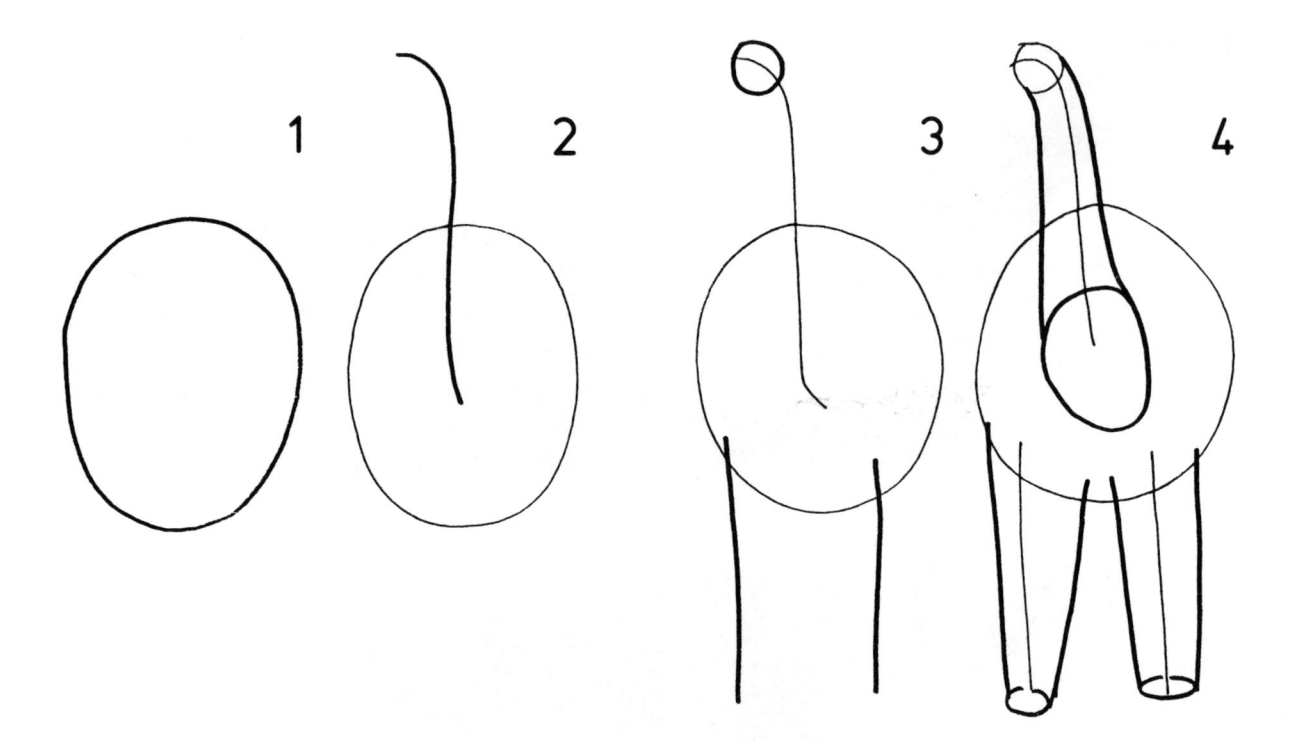

Scientists have found lots of bones that belonged to this huge dinosaur. But they can only guess what its head must have been like. Mary has chosen to draw the head as if it were a **Brachiosaurus** (brack-ee-oh-saw-rus) which you can see on page 25.

Keep the tones you use strong and dark for this enormous creature as it walks towards you. Look how thick its legs are – just like an elephant's.

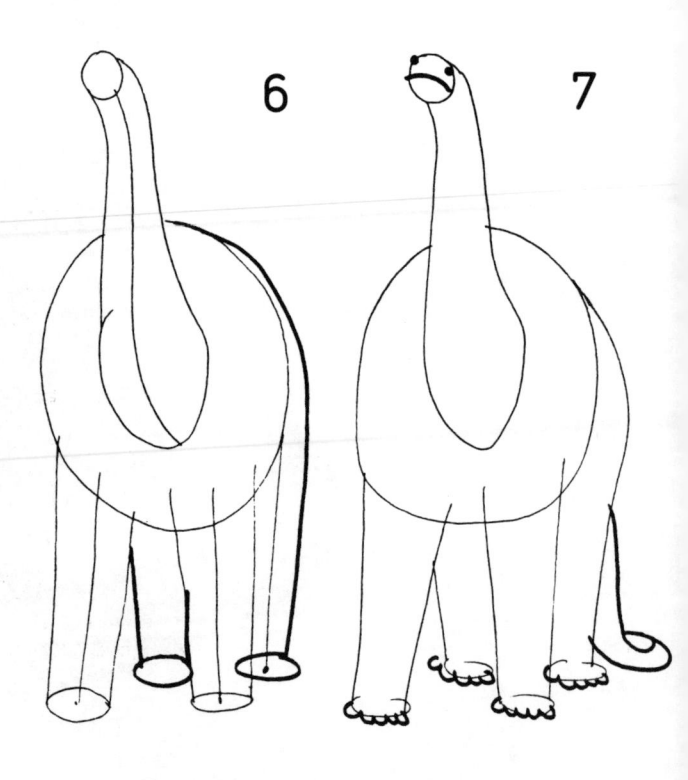

115

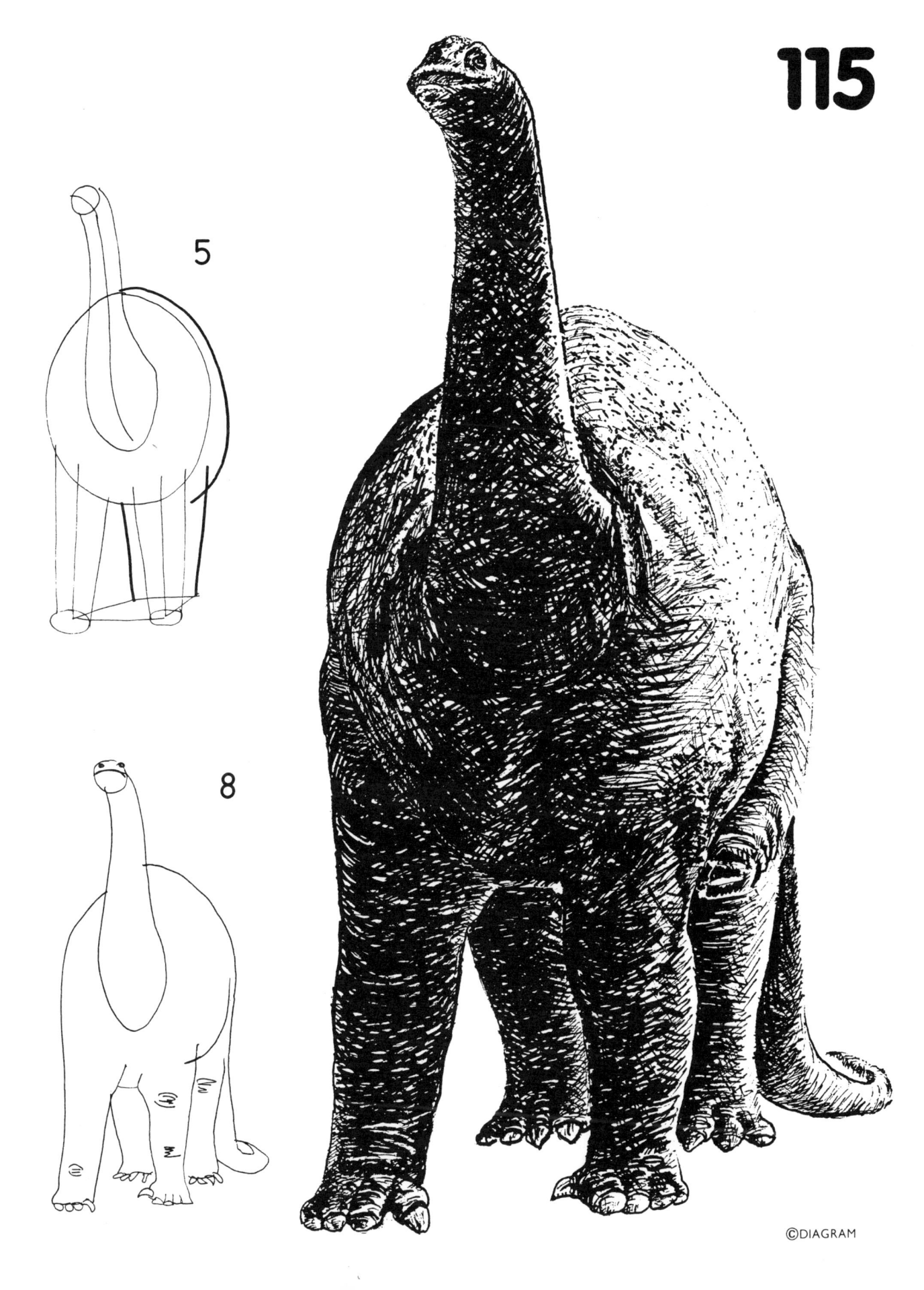

5

8

Mamenchisaurus
(ma-men-chee-saw-rus)

Of all the dinosaurs, this one probably has the oddest shape. At the bottom of the next page I have drawn a side view so you can see the enormous length of the neck and tail. (It must have been very unhappy if it got a cold and a sore throat!)

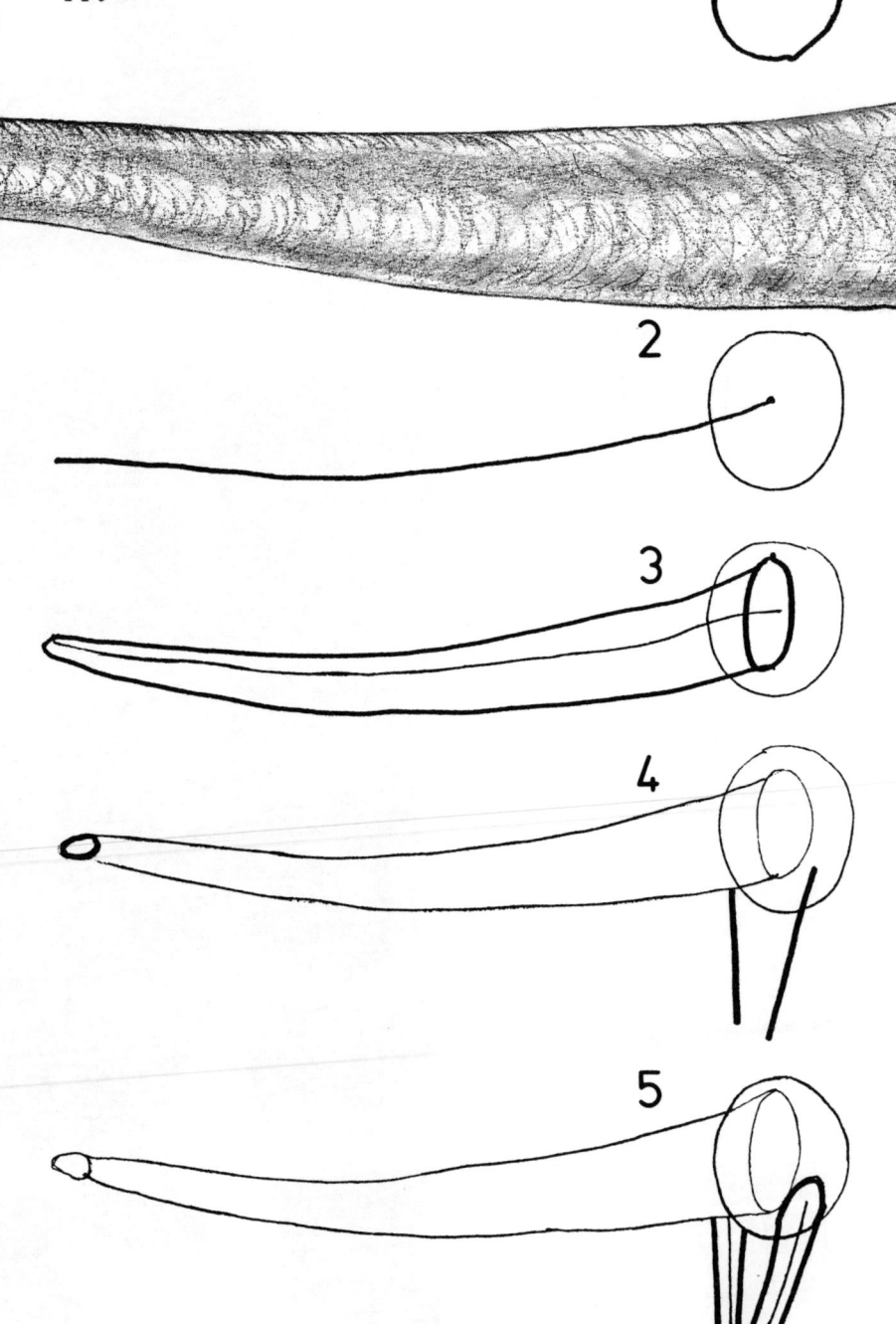

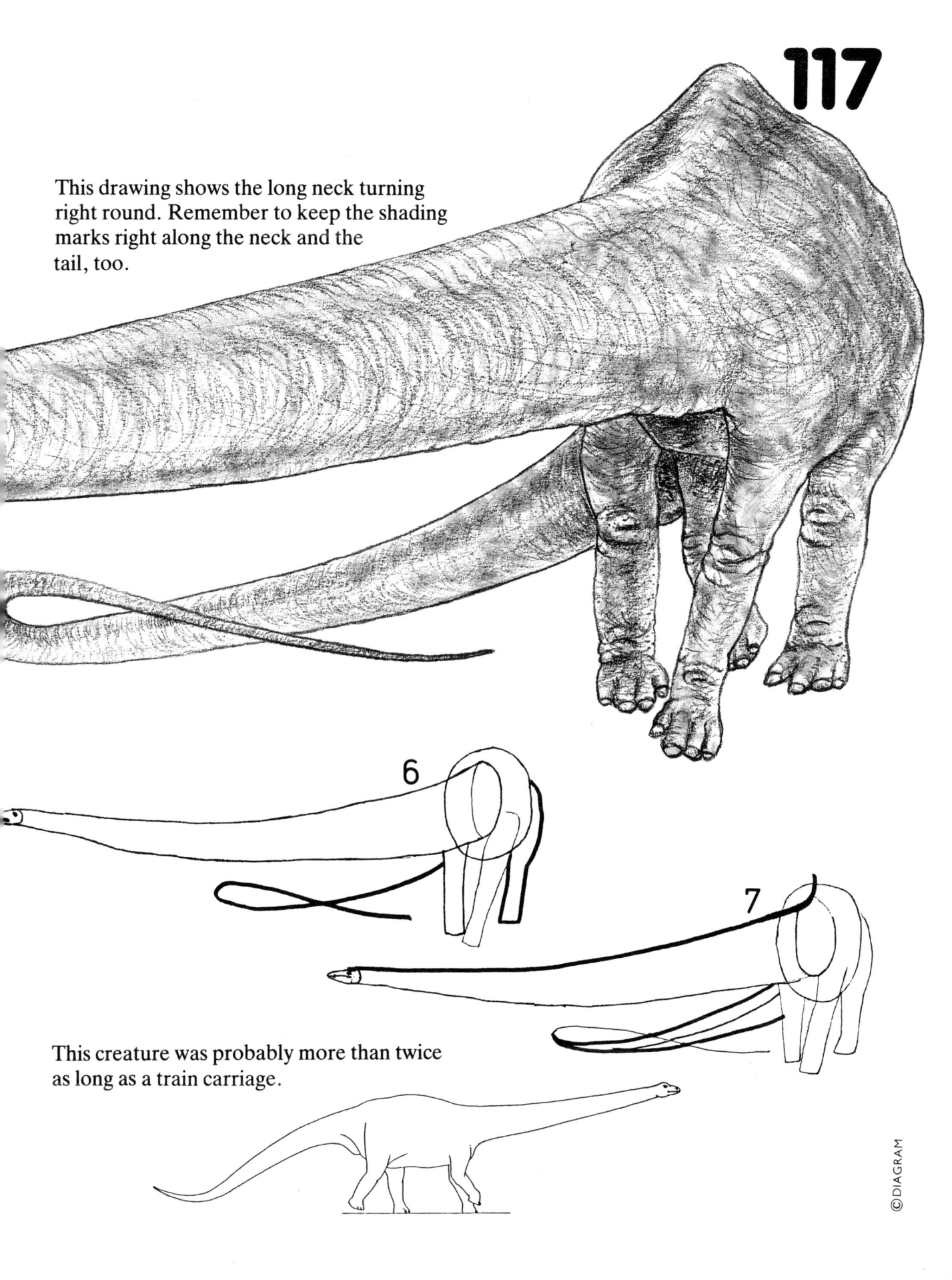

This drawing shows the long neck turning right round. Remember to keep the shading marks right along the neck and the tail, too.

117

6

7

This creature was probably more than twice as long as a train carriage.

©DIAGRAM

Pteranodon (ter-an-oh-don)

This was a giant bat-like monster, about the same size as a small airplane. It would swoop down over open spaces looking for small creatures it could snap up for food.

Begin your drawing by sketching a simple flat view of the creature, as shown here. When you can draw all the parts in the right way, try to make a picture of the creature in flight, swooping down towards you.

You can also add a flying monster like this one to any of your other dinosaur pictures as part of the background.

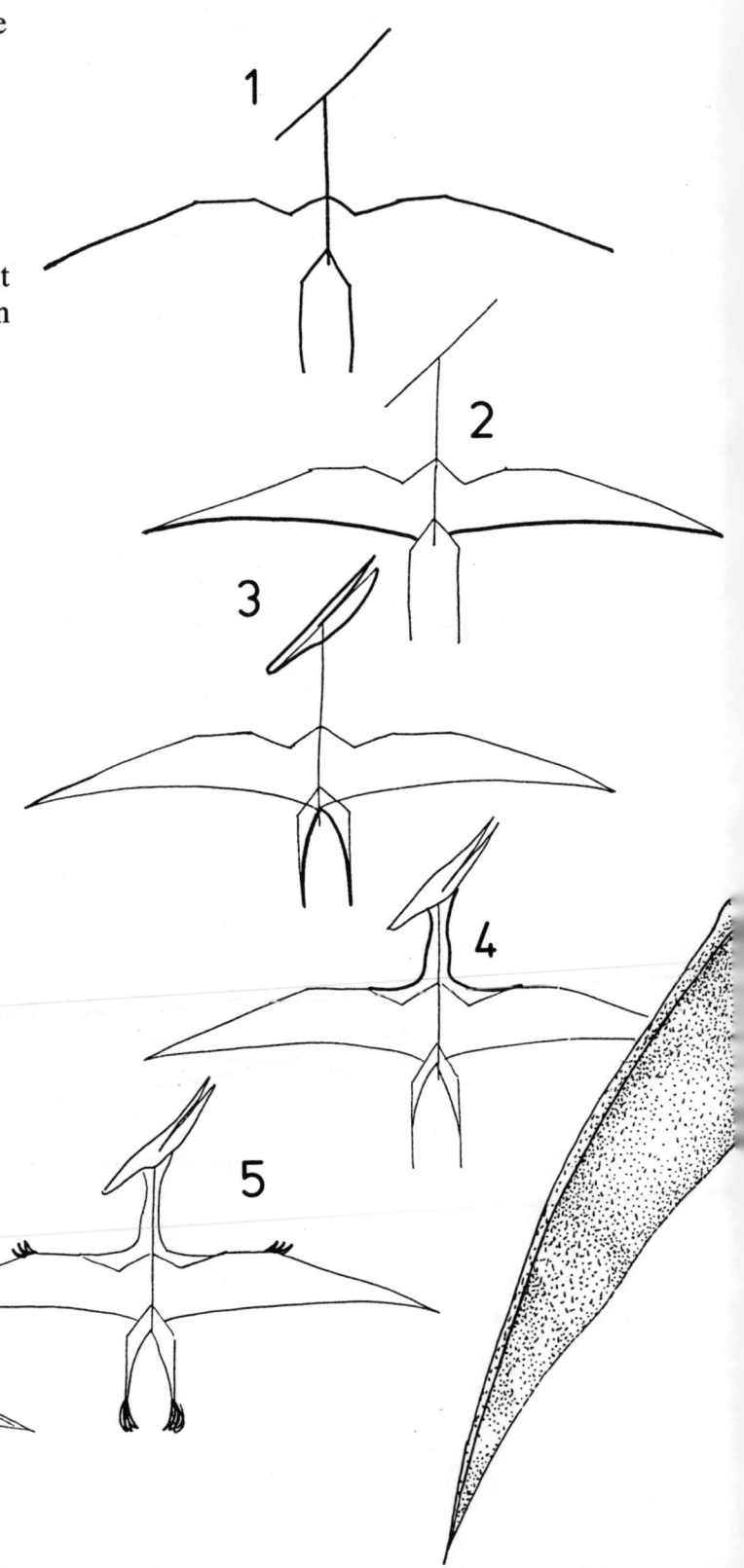

119

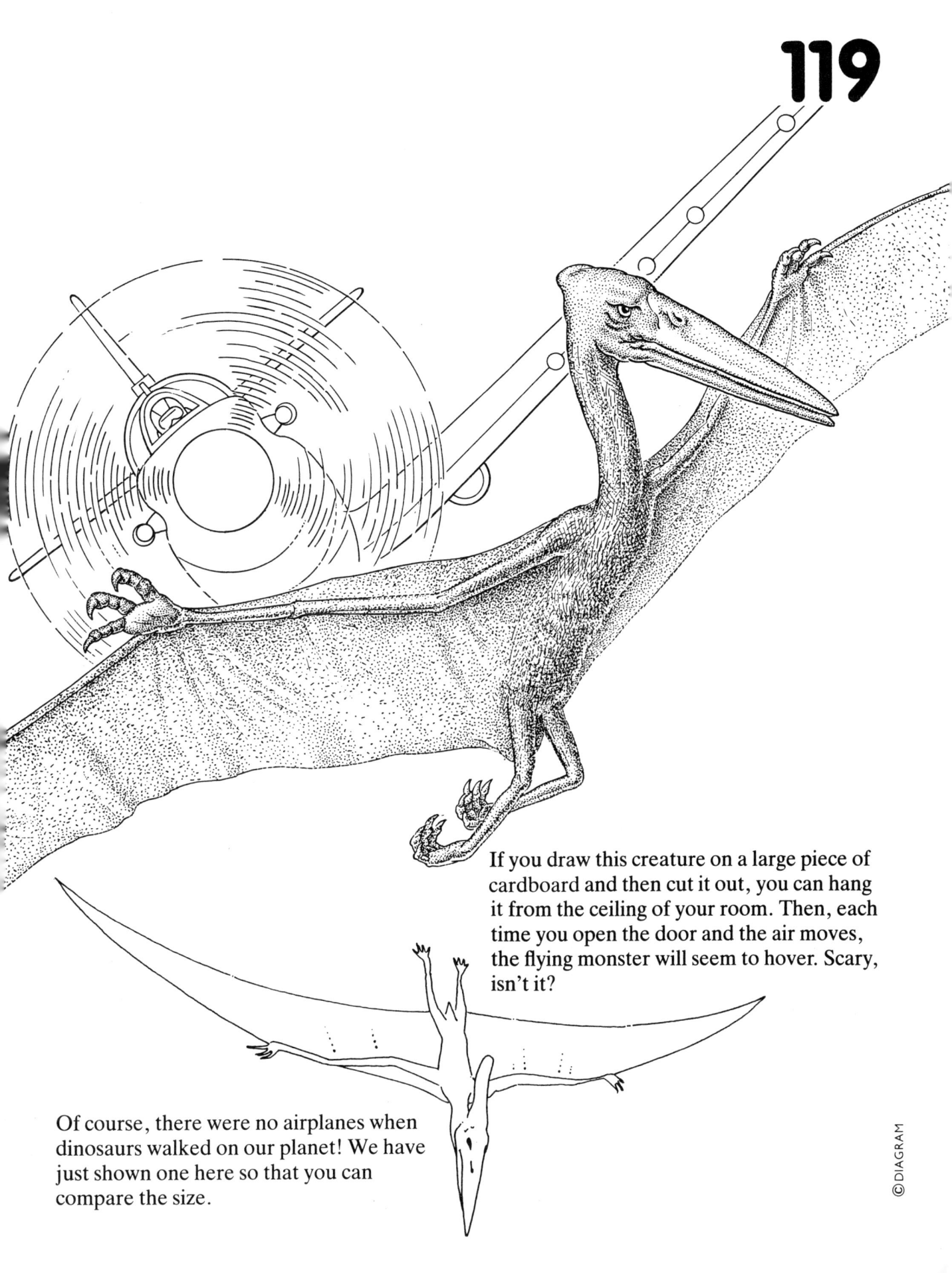

If you draw this creature on a large piece of cardboard and then cut it out, you can hang it from the ceiling of your room. Then, each time you open the door and the air moves, the flying monster will seem to hover. Scary, isn't it?

Of course, there were no airplanes when dinosaurs walked on our planet! We have just shown one here so that you can compare the size.

©DIAGRAM

Parasaurolophus
(para-saw-roll-loaf-us)

This creature, which ate grass or leaves, had a long nose that pointed backward from its head. Some scientists think it used this to make trumpet sounds. But others think that this nose was larger in males and that it was used to attract the females or for head-banging in fights with other males.

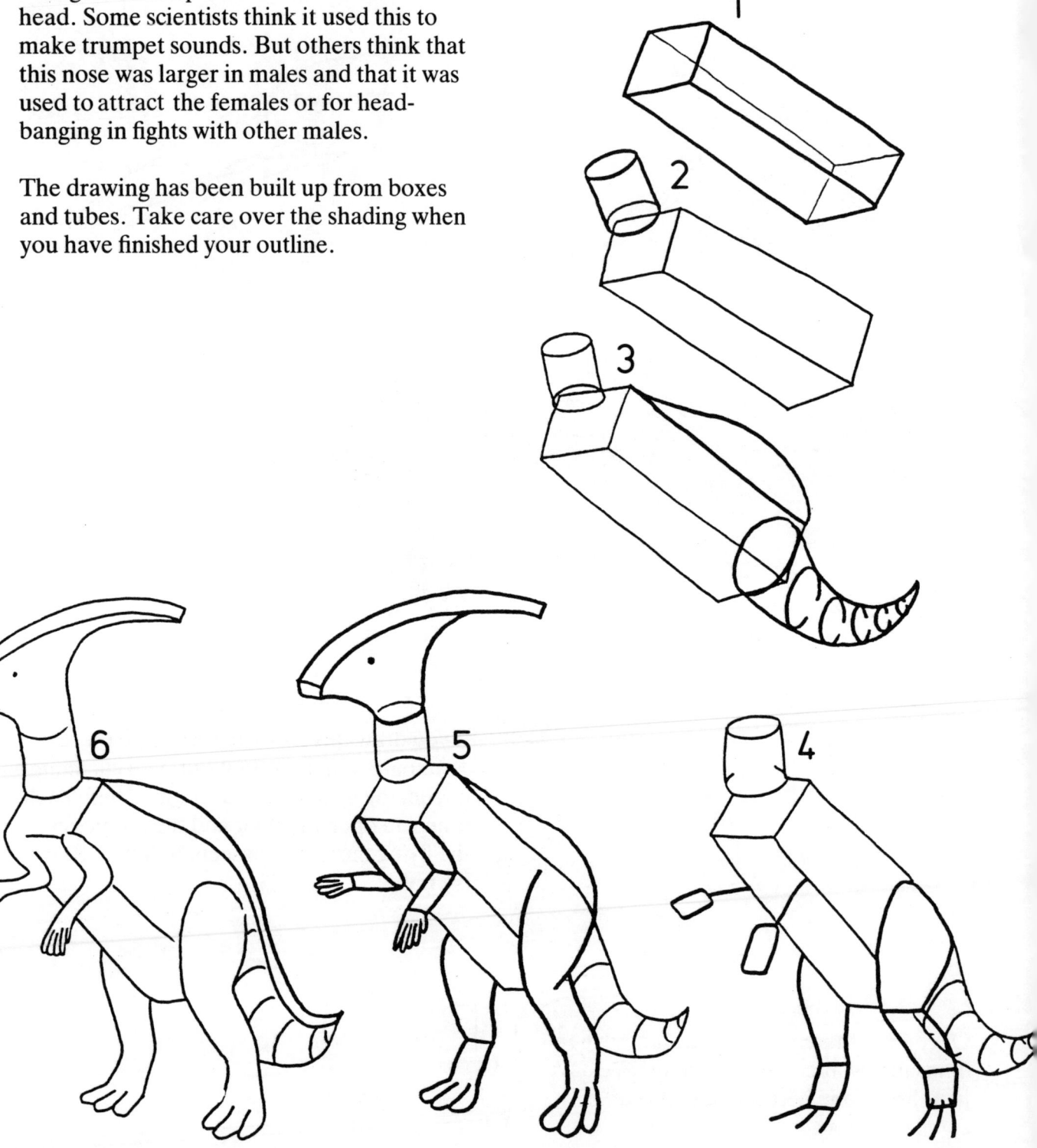

The drawing has been built up from boxes and tubes. Take care over the shading when you have finished your outline.

121

This **Parasaurolophus** had a cousin called a **Lambeosaurus**. You can meet this creature on page 126.

Megalosaurus (meg-a-low-saw-rus)

This dinosaur looked a little like the **Parasaurolophus** (para-saw-roll-loaf-us) on the previous page. But it was a meat-eating monster. Its cousin – the **Tyrannosaurus** (tie-ran-oh-saw-rus) – was the most frightening creature you could possibly imagine.

Turn to page 58 if you would like to see the skeleton of the **Megalosaurus**. (Look to the top of the page to find out how to say its name if you are not quite sure.) Notice how long its tail is, and how short its arms are.

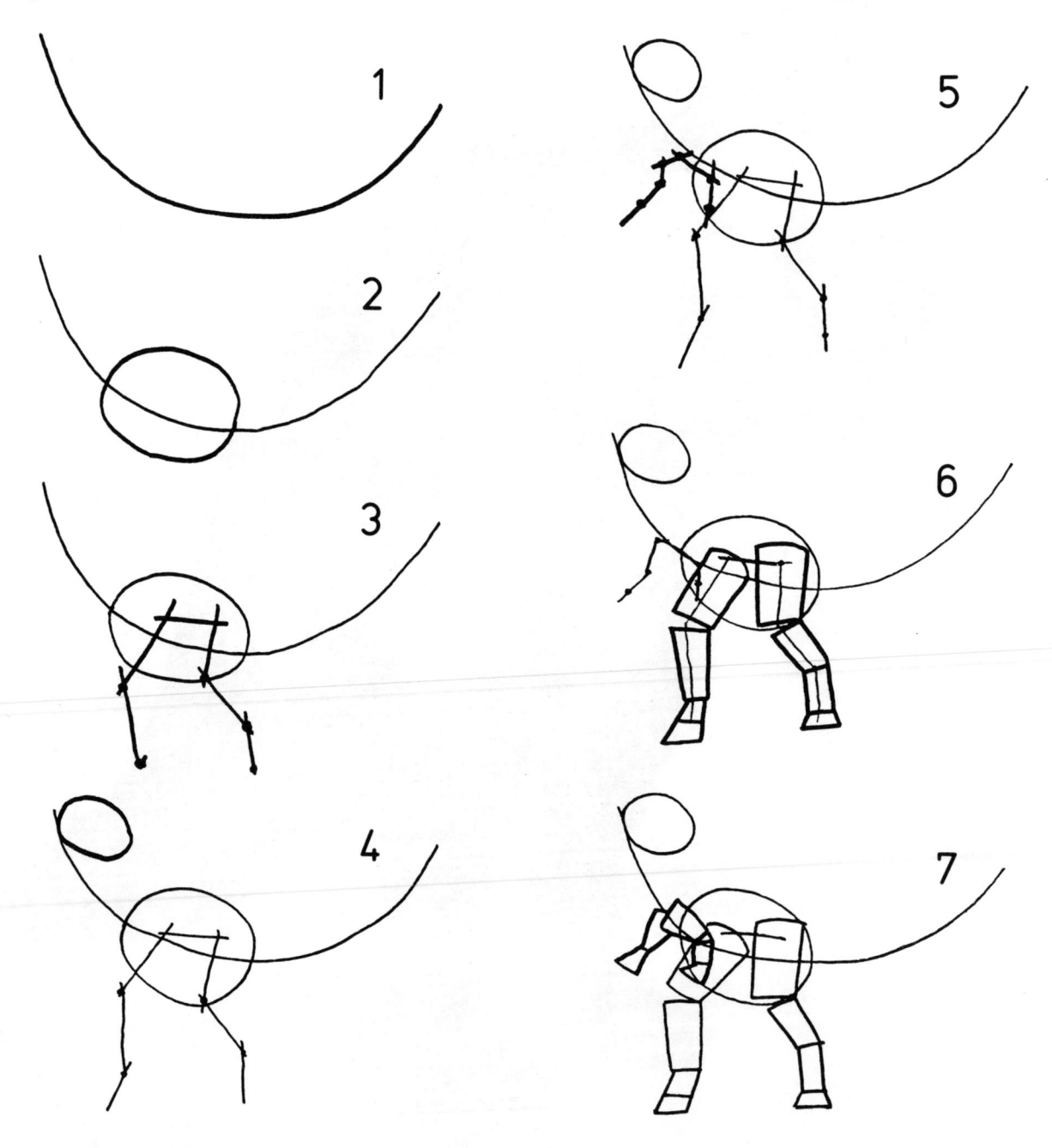

123

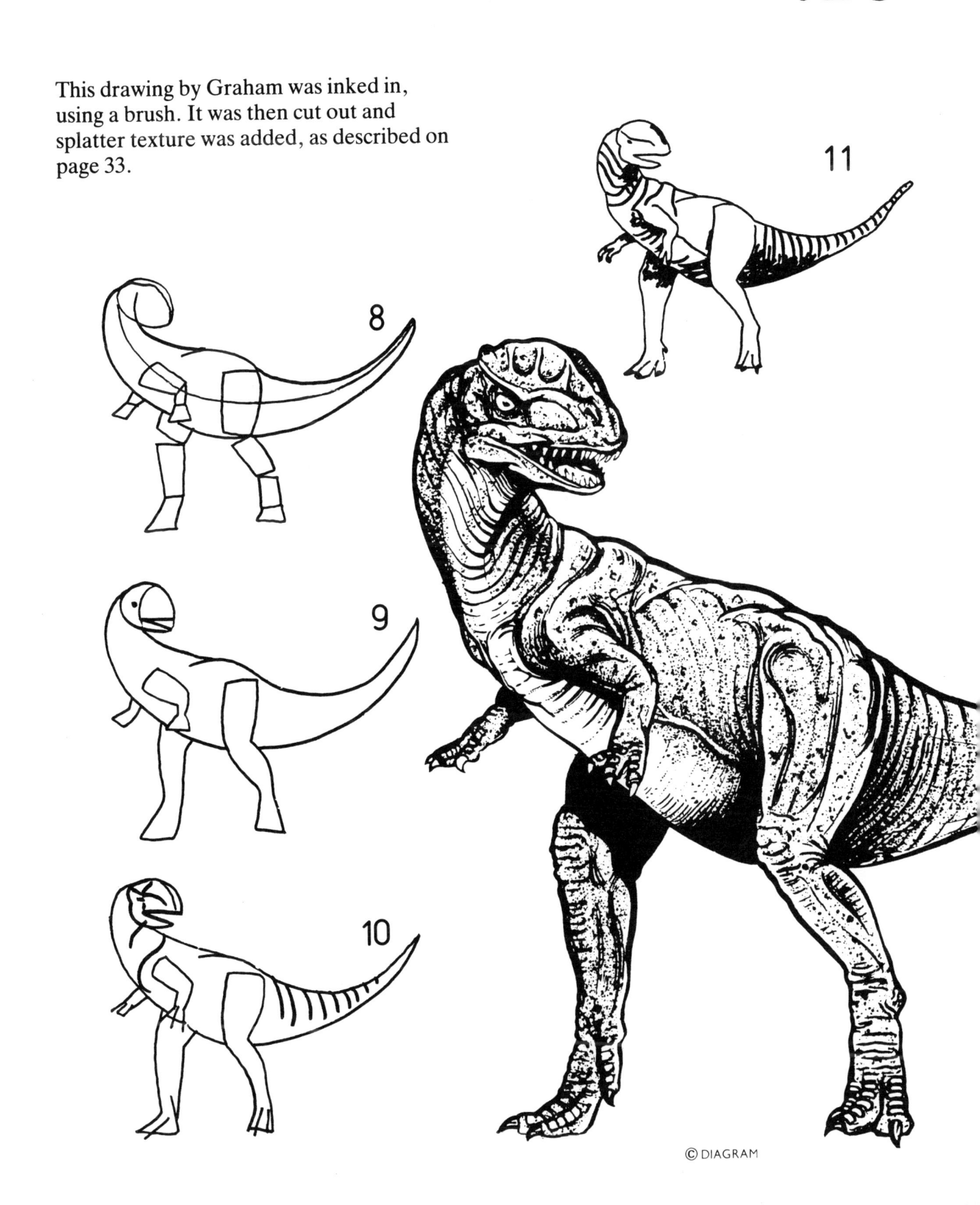

This drawing by Graham was inked in, using a brush. It was then cut out and splatter texture was added, as described on page 33.

8

9

10

11

©DIAGRAM

Tyrannosaurus (tie-ran-oh-saw-rus)

On these two pages, you can see how to build up a drawing of this terrifying meat-eating monster from a series of tin can shapes.

It might look most frightening if you drew it in felt-tips.

Look back to page 100 to see what its skeleton was like.

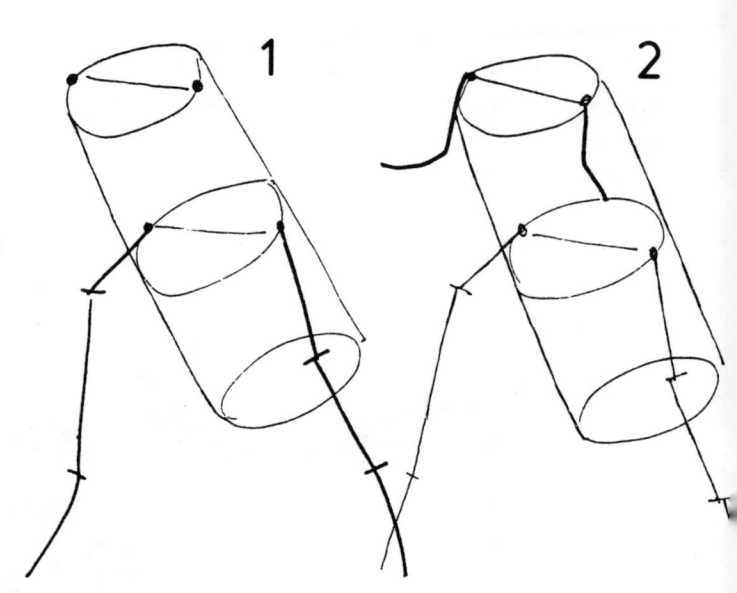

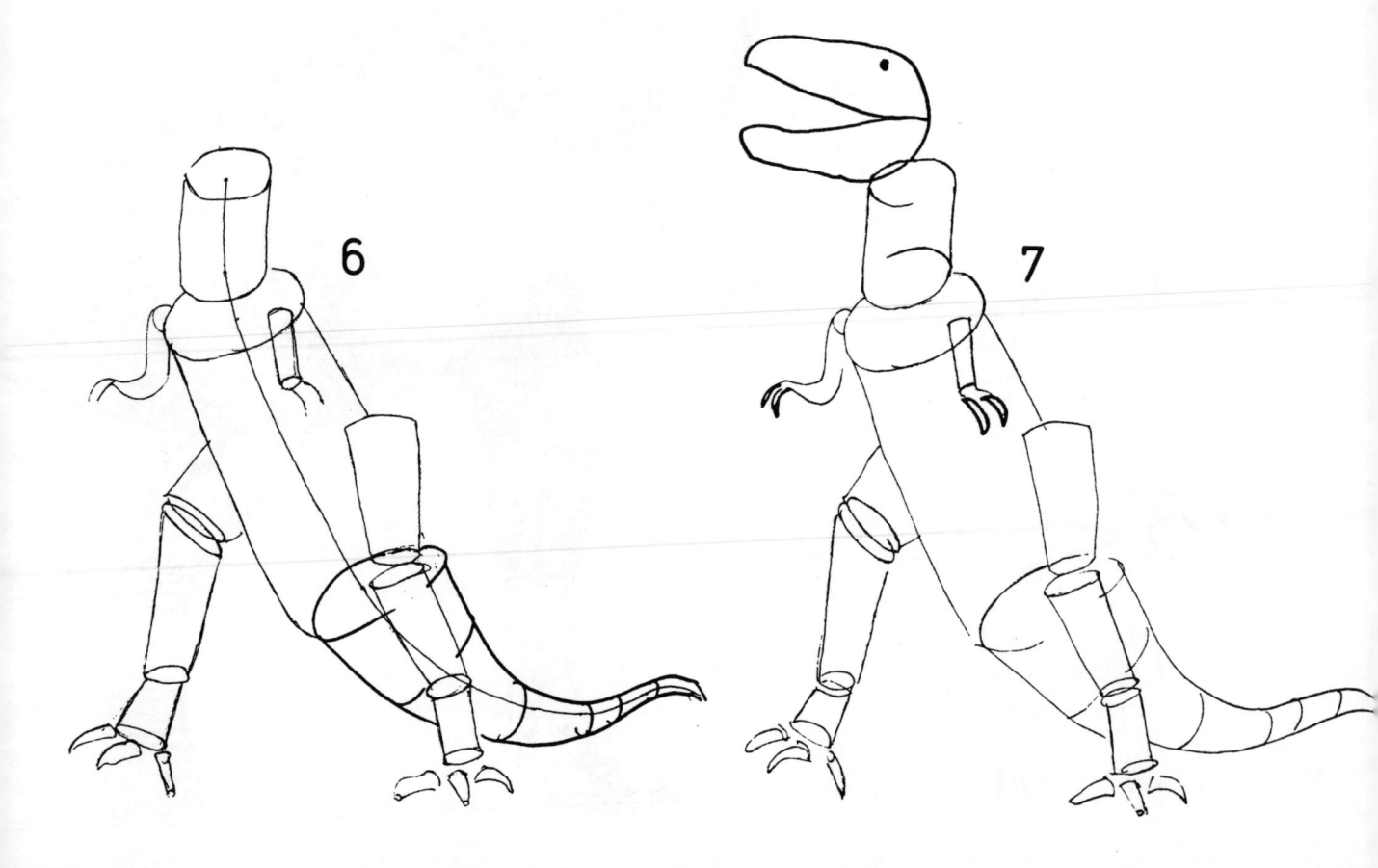

125

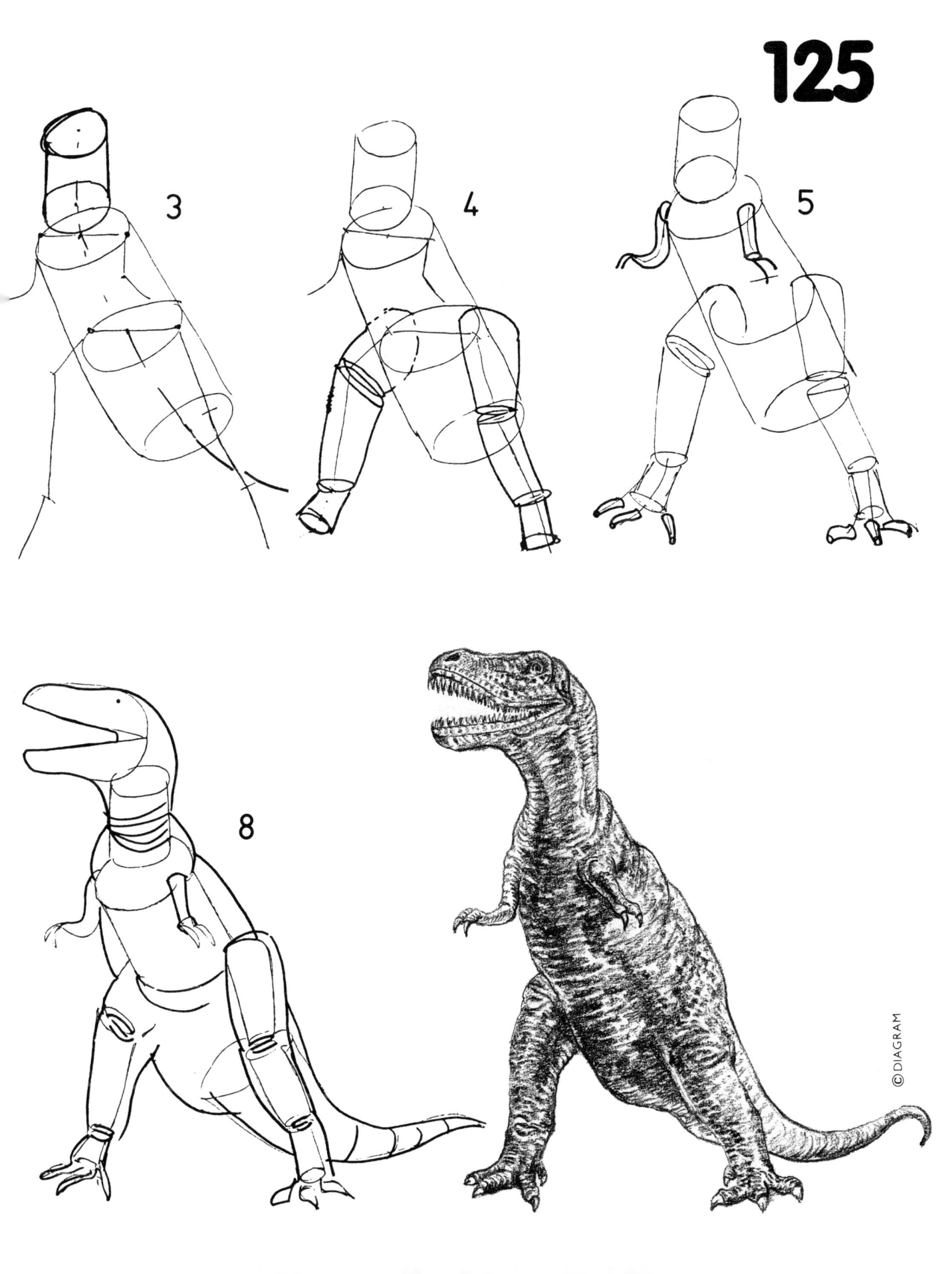

Lambeosaurus
(lamb-ee-oh-saw-rus)

Some creatures like the **Lambeosaurus** shown here and its cousin, the **Parasaurolophus**, on page 121, had differently shaped heads. Scientists think it may have been to help them tell which were male and which were female.

Drawing their heads is a little like drawing the head of a horse. Begin with an egg shape at an angle. Then build up the details. Remember that the position of the eyes, ears and nostrils must balance if you see both in your drawing.

127

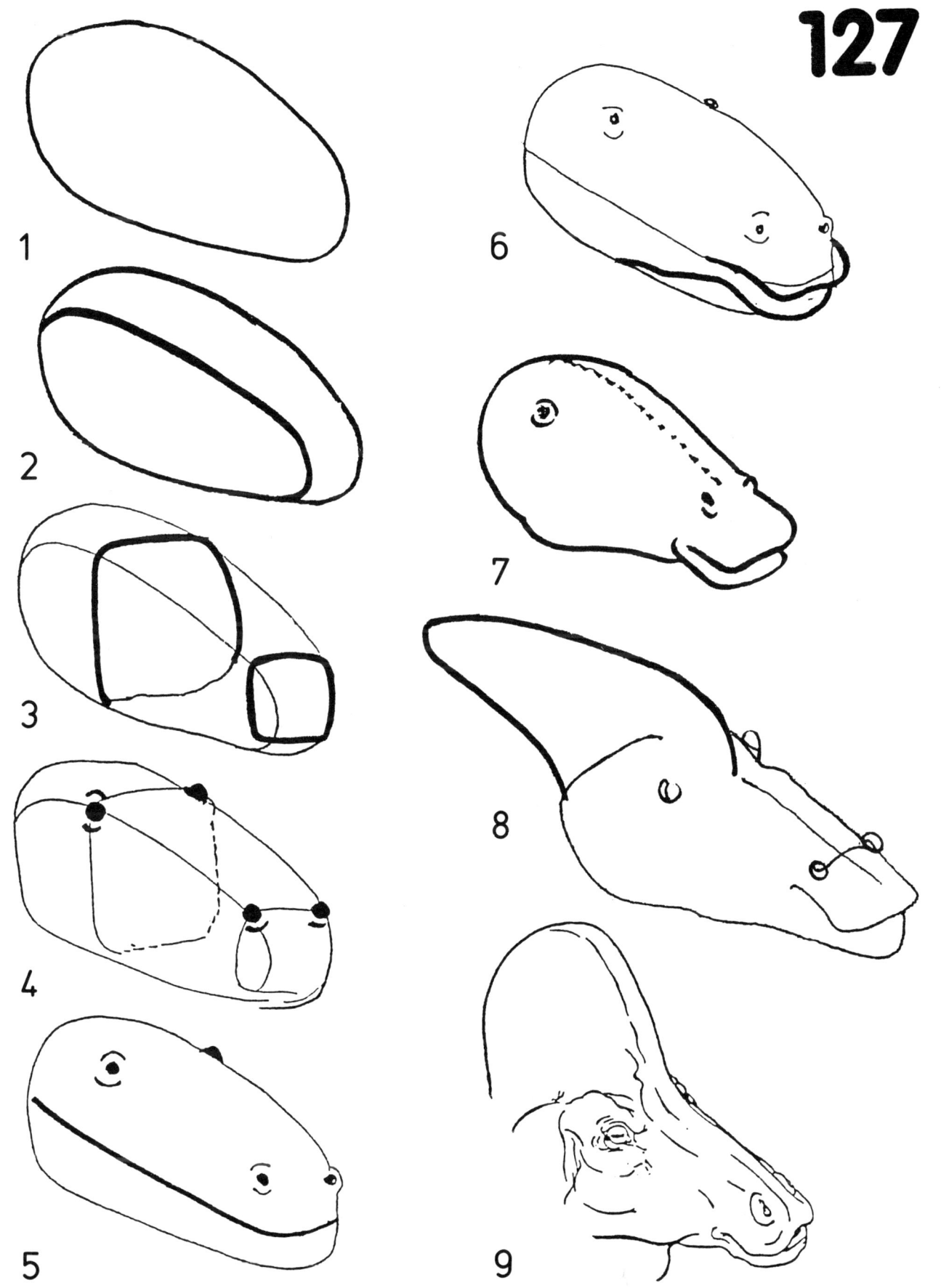

Stegosaurus (steg-oh-saw-rus) rear side view

This creature has its back to us, and is also slightly to the side. Before you start to copy it, take a look at the simple side view on page 41 and also page 103.

It will help to make the dinosaur seem to be walking away if you shade the nearest parts of its body darker than those that are farther away from you. This means the nose should be faint but the tail should be very black or a deep tone of any other shade you choose to use.

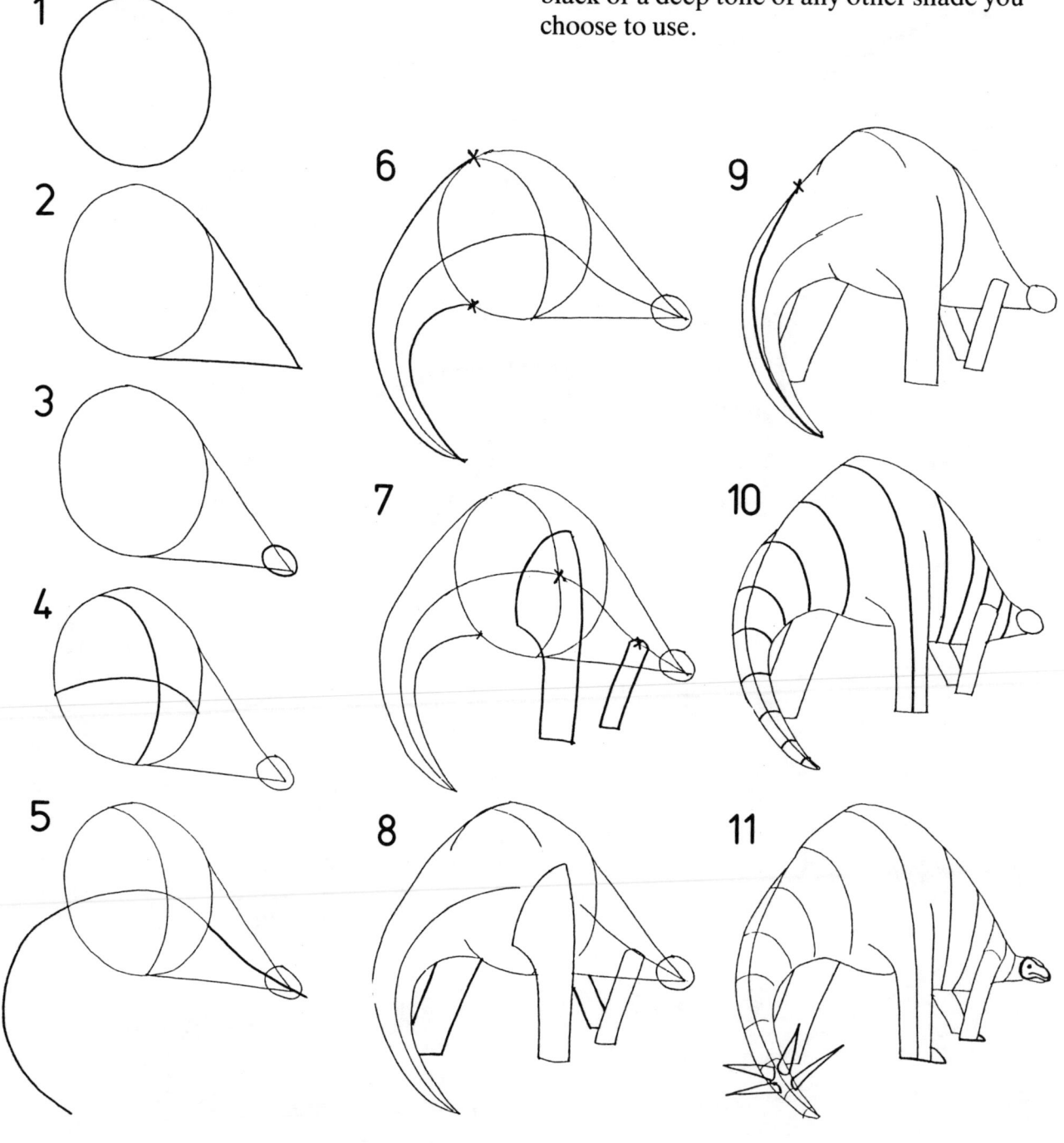

129

12

13

Stenonychosaurus
(sten-on-itch-oh-saw-rus)

To help you build up this dinosaur's body, I suggest you begin to plan this picture in pencil first. When you add the detail on the skin, think of the wrinkles as pieces of string wrapped around the creature's body.
And don't forget to add the beady eyes.

Some say this was probably the most intelligent of all the dinosaurs. It could also run very fast on its thin legs.

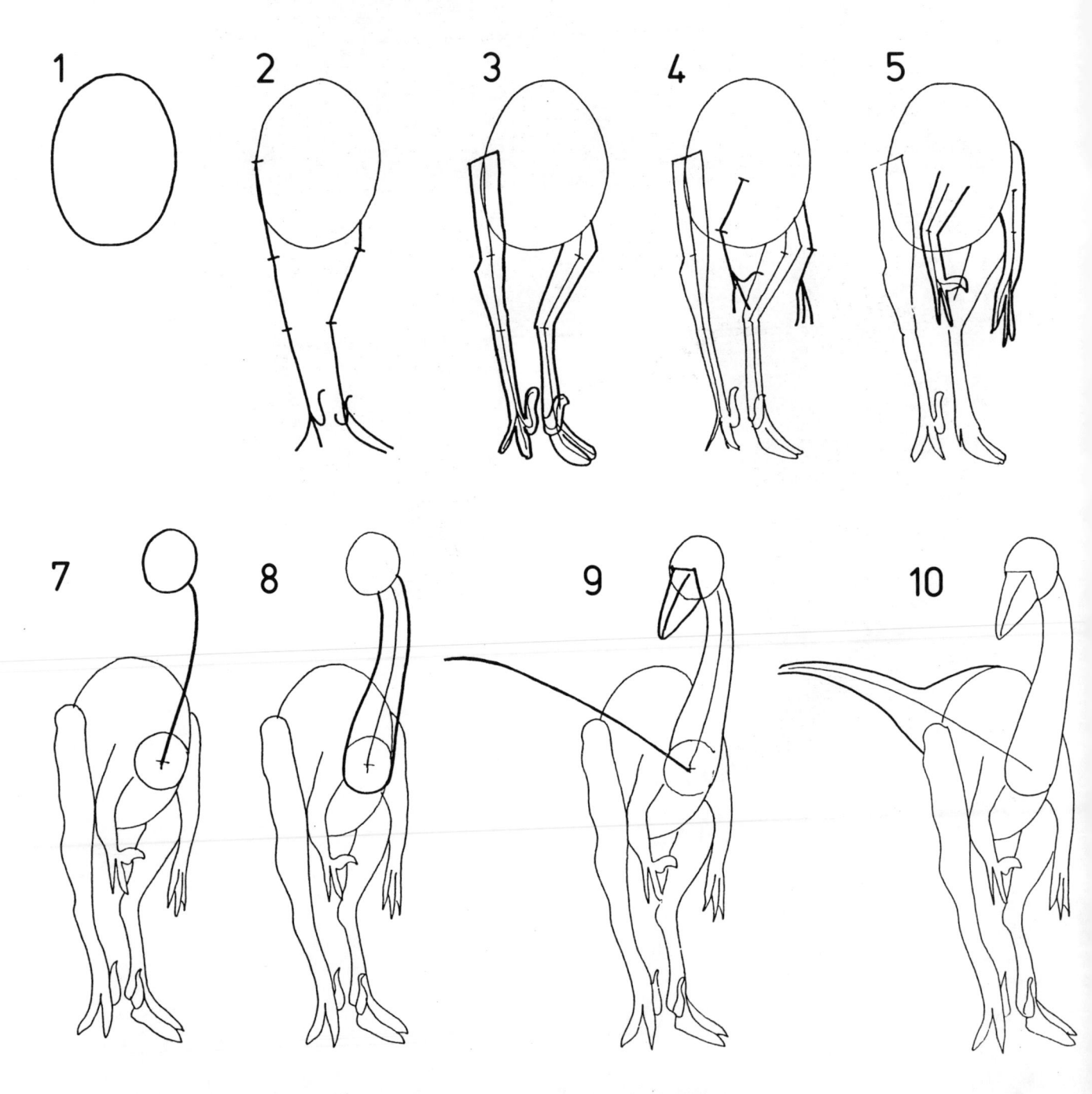

131

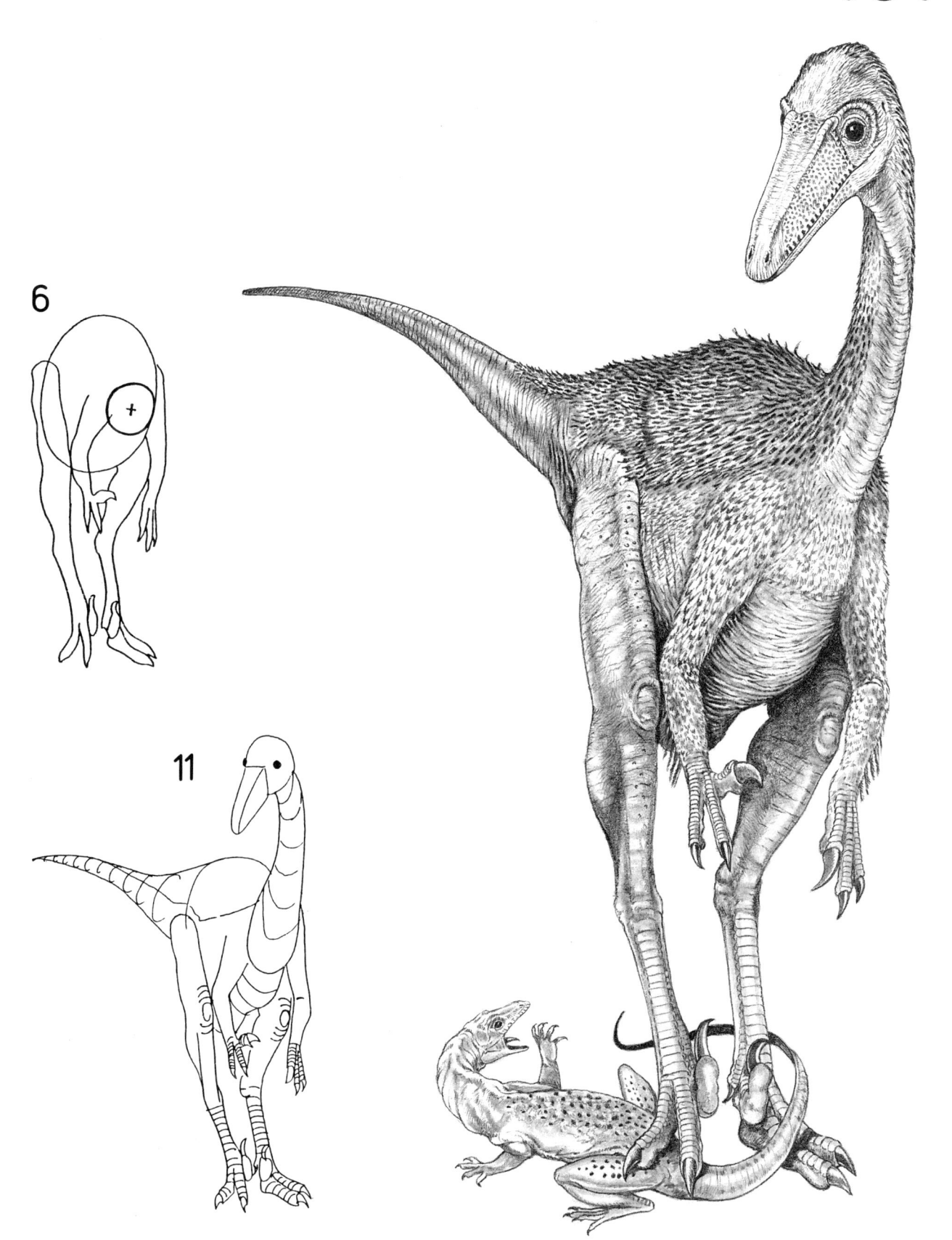

6

11

Dimetrodon (di-met-roh-don)

This creature was a sort of giant lizard with a sail-like fin on its back. Before you begin this drawing, look at the other pictures of the beast on pages 39 and 51. It will help you to understand its basic shape.

Perhaps use a felt-tip to bring your drawing to life, and then add all the detail with a ballpoint pen. Notice all the ridges that run up the fin on its back, and all the dots and lines that show how scaly the creature probably was.

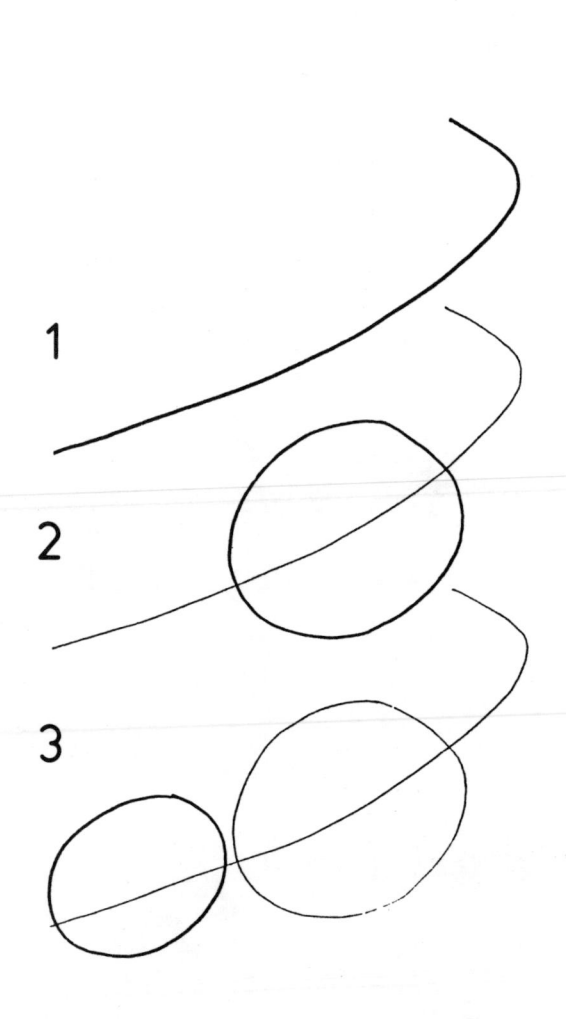

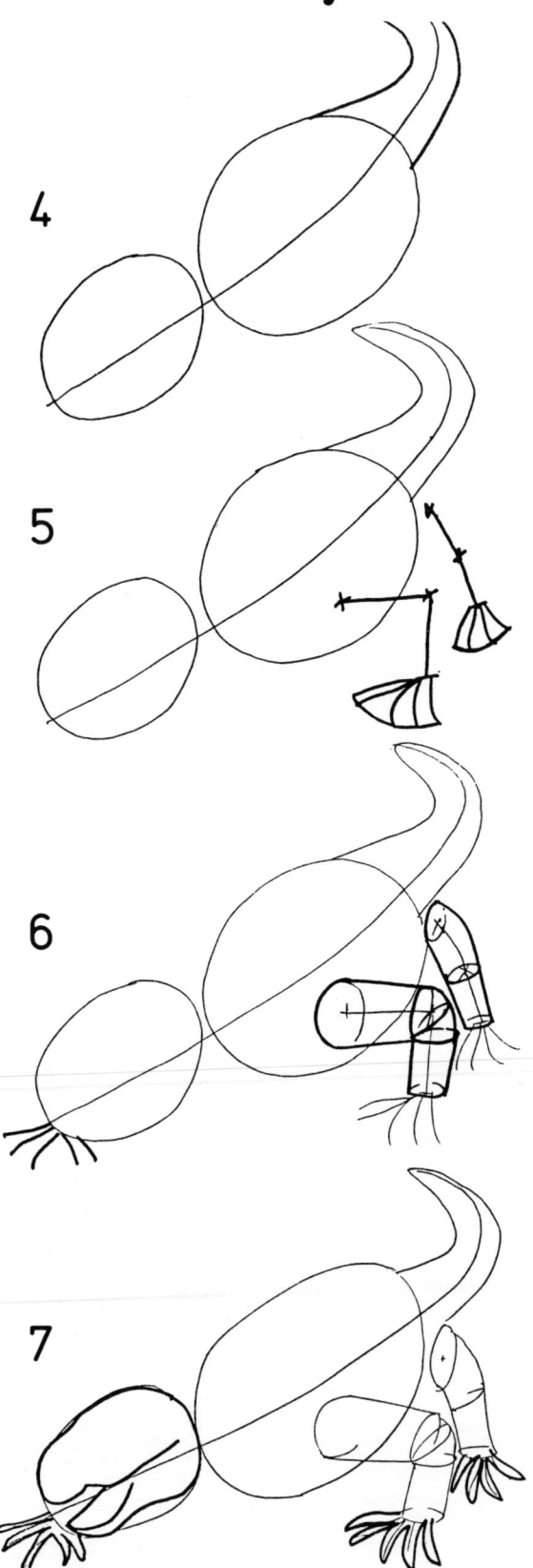

1

2

3

4

5

6

7

133

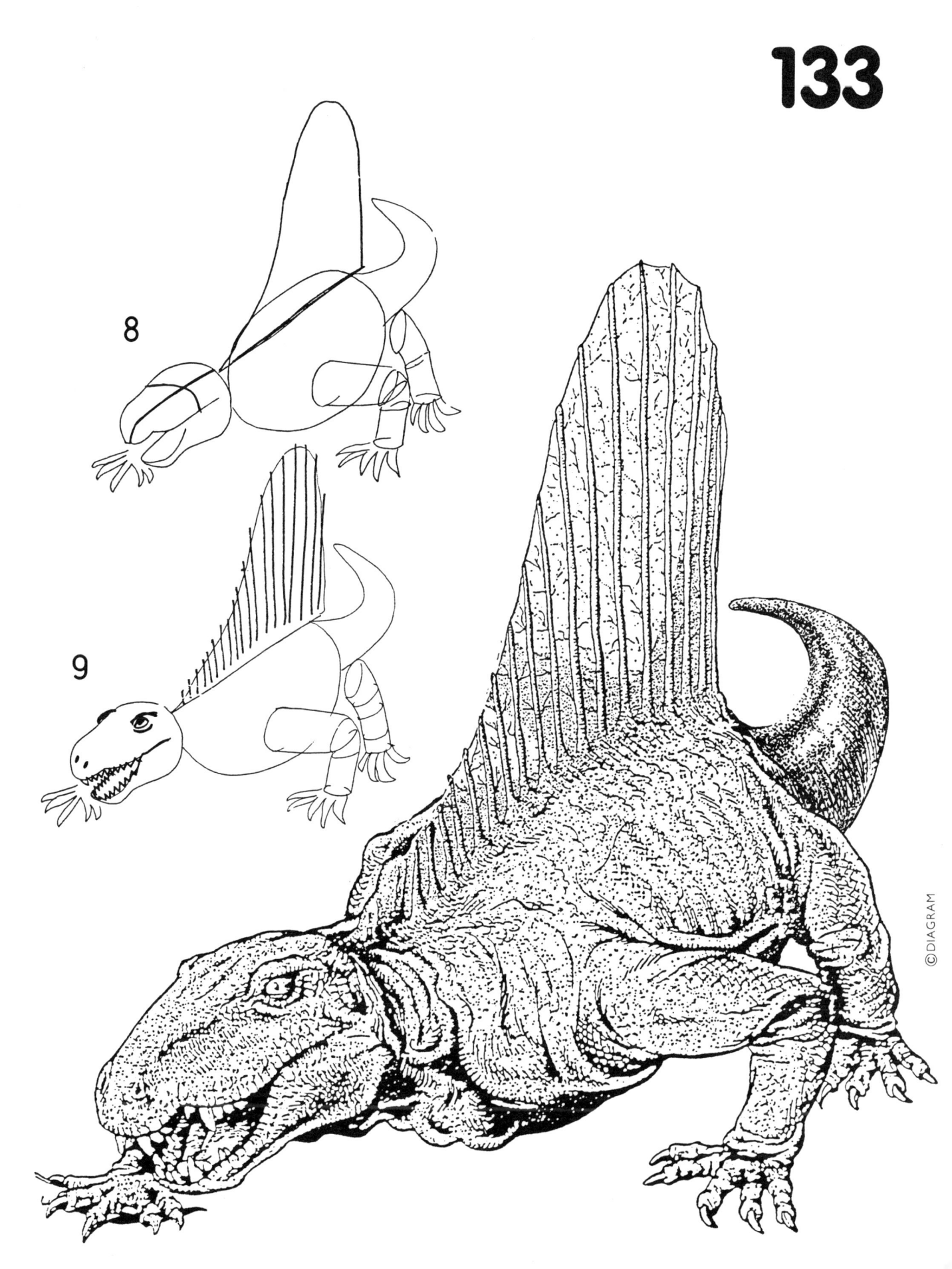

8

9

Dryptosaurus (drip-toe-saw-rus)

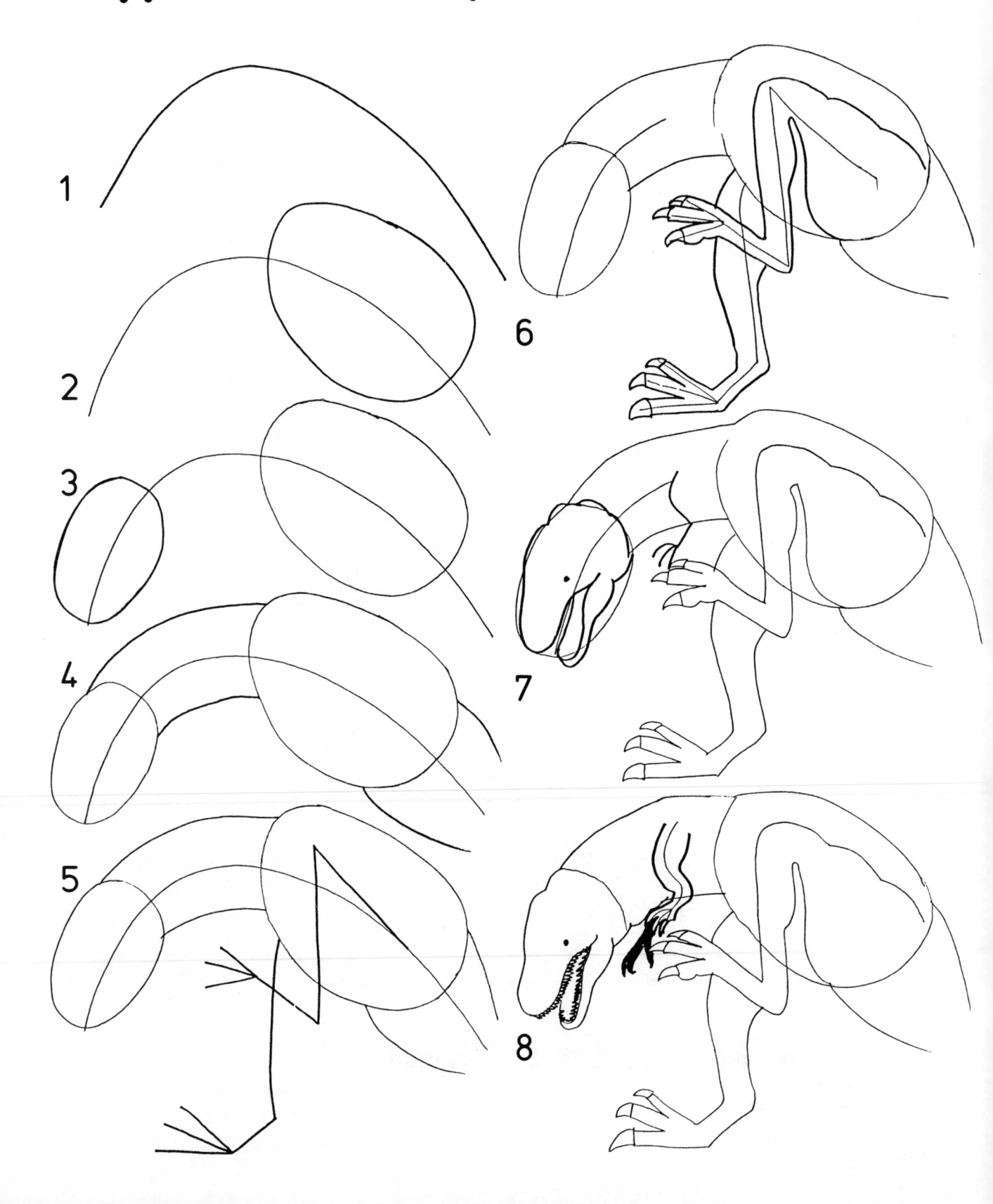

1
2
3
4
5
6
7
8

135

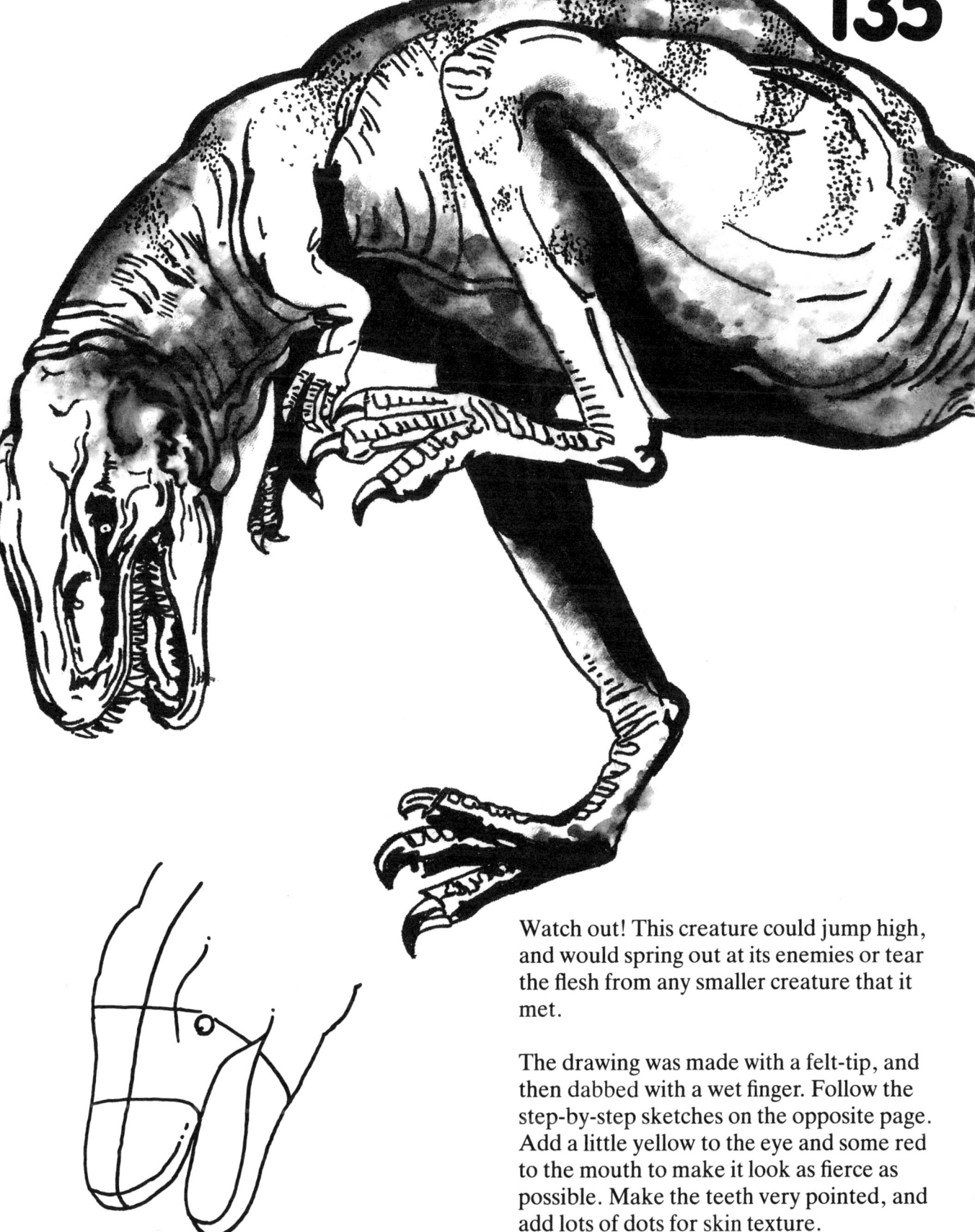

Watch out! This creature could jump high, and would spring out at its enemies or tear the flesh from any smaller creature that it met.

The drawing was made with a felt-tip, and then dabbed with a wet finger. Follow the step-by-step sketches on the opposite page. Add a little yellow to the eye and some red to the mouth to make it look as fierce as possible. Make the teeth very pointed, and add lots of dots for skin texture.

© DIAGRAM

Protoceratops (pro-to-ser-a-tops)

Now that you have drawn so many dinosaurs on their own, you may like to draw two or even three together, and add some background. This drawing is of two fierce creatures, face-to-face.

Follow the step-by-step sketches for the creature that is facing you. Then try to work out your own step-by-step sketches for the rear view of the other beast.

Make their eyes really gleam in a frightening way by adding a spot of white to the black pupils.

137

Creating your own dinosaurs

Have some fun inventing your own dinosaurs, and perhaps give them some amazing names, too, just as Ryozo has done here. This is your chance to start drawing some of the wildest creatures you could possibly imagine!

Scientists have worked out what all the different kinds of dinosaur probably looked like from the bones they have found. But there may have been other types with skeletons that have not yet been discovered.

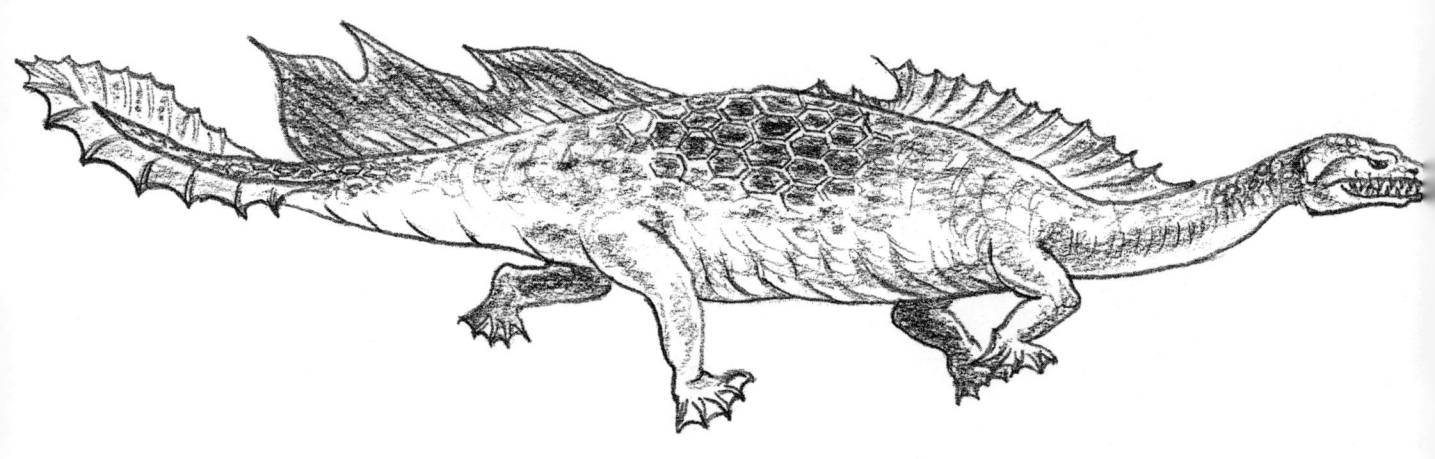

Centasaurus (sent-a-saw-rus)

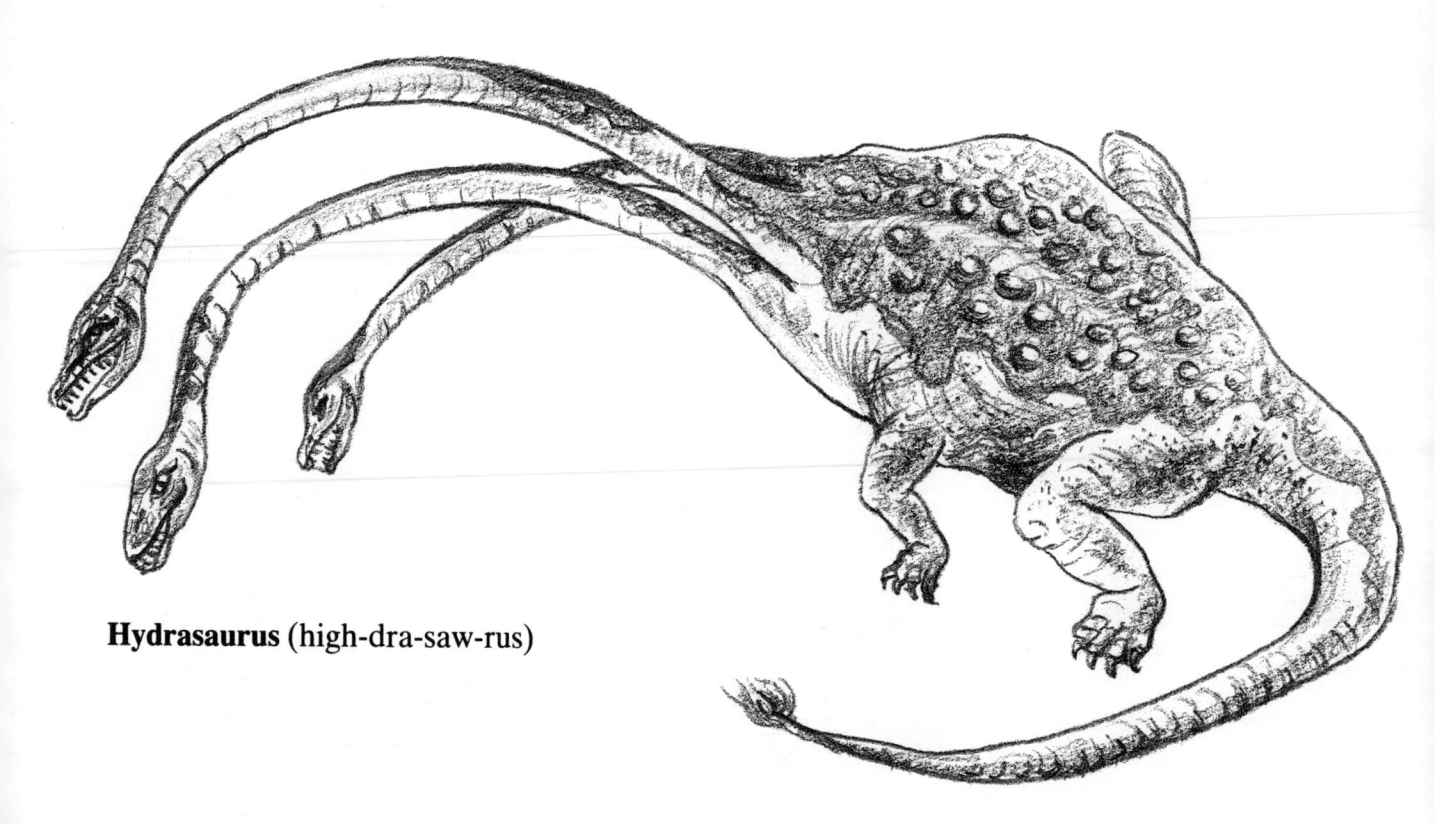

Hydrasaurus (high-dra-saw-rus)

The head of a **Campylodonasus** (camp-ill-odd-on-as-us)

Hexaceratops (hecks-ass-sir-a-tops)

Remember, you cannot find any of the creatures on these two pages in any other books on dinosaurs. They are all fantasy beasts with imaginary names.

These squares can be used for enlarging your drawings, as described on page 42.

Index

Apatosaurus 14–15
Archaeopteryx 14–15, 106–107
Avimimus 54

Ballpoint pen 29
Birthday cards 45
Bones 9, 47
Brachiosaurus 17, 24, 25, 110–111
Brushes 30–31

Caenagnathus 19
Cards 45
Chalks 26–27
Charcoal 26–27
Claws 9
Comics 45
Compsognathus 14–15
Copying 40–41
Corythosaurus 38
Crayons 26–27, 34, 34–35
Cretaceous age 17

Dabbing 33
Deinonychus 26–27
Dilophosaurus 72–73
Dimetrodon 38–39, 51, 132–133
Dip pens 28
Diplodocus 50, 57, 62–63, 68–69, 74–75
Dots 48–49
Drawing pads 37
Dromiceimimus 51, 57, 86–87
Dryptosaurus 46–47, 134–135
Dunkleosteus 92–93

Eggs 12, 95
Enlarging 42–43, 140
Environment 9
Euoplocephalus 14–15

Feathers 13, 54
Felt-tip pens 29
Food 12
Footprints 9
Fossils 9
Fountain pens 28
Frieze 44

Greeting cards 45

Horns 13

Icarosaurus 90–91
Ink 28–29, 30–31
Invitations 45

Join the dots 48–49
Jurassic age 16

Lambeosaurus 121, 126–127
Light 21

Mamenchisaurus 116–117
Mammuthus primigenius 51, 80–81
Meat-eating dinosaurs 12
Megalosaurus 28–29, 58, 122–123
Megatherium 50, 76–77, 78
Mobiles 44
Movement 56–57

Ouranosaurus 59

Pachycephalosaurus 14–15
Paints 30–31
Paper 36–37
Parasaurolophus 14–15, 64, 120–121, 126
Pastels 26
Pencils 24–25
Pens 28–29
Phorusrhacos longissimus 108–109
Placodus 98–99
Plant-eating dinosaurs 12–13
Plateosaurus 65, 112–113, 114–115
Plesiosaur 50, 65, 94–95
Probactrosaurus 8
Projects 44–45
Protoceratops 136–137
Pteranodon 65, 118–119

Quetzalcoatlus 14–15

Research 45
Rubbing out 24

Sarcosaurus 47, 88–89
Saurolophus 55
Scales 13
Scrapbooks 45
Scraping 33
Shapes 46, 50–51
Shells 13, 54

Silhouettes 50–51, 52–53
Size 14–15
Skeletons 8–9, 47, 57, 58–59, 100–101
Skin 12–13, 54–55
see also Textures
Smilodon 60, 78–79
Smudging 26, 32
Softening 33
Soluble paints 34–35
Special effects 34–35
Space 20
Speed 12
Spinosaurus 46, 84–85
Spikes 13
Splattering 33
Squares for copying 140
Staurikosaurus 16
Stegosaurus 14–15, 41, 51, 64, 102–103, 128–129
Stencils 44
Stenonychosaurus 63, 130–131
Step-by-step 72–73
Struthiosaurus 63, 104–105
Stick dinosaurs 56–57

Teeth 9
Tenontosaurus 26–27
Textures 32–33, 54–55
Time-ribbon 10–11
Tin-can dinosaurs 60–61
Torosaurus 51, 82–83
Tracing 38–39
Tracing paper 37
Transferring tracings 38–39
Triassic age 16
Triceratops 14–15, 17, 59
Tylosaurus 96–97
Tyrannosaurus 14–15, 17, 38, 100–101, 122, 124–125

Using your drawings 44–45

Vegetarian dinosaurs 12–13
Velociraptor 14
Viewpoint 62–63

Wax crayons 26–27, 34–35

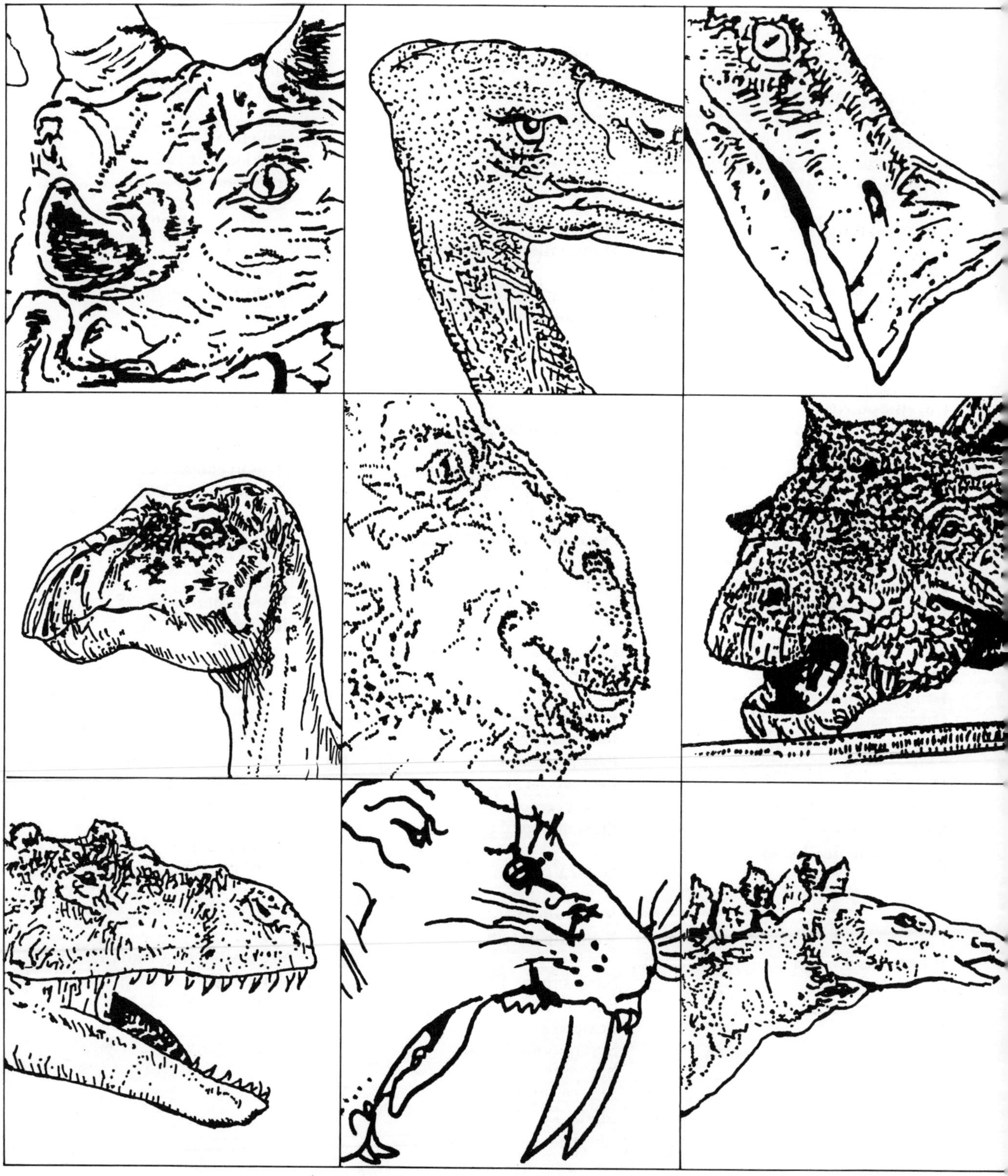

Here and at the front of the book are details from some of the drawings featured. Can you find the pages on which they appear?